FORWARD

It was while I was working in a local care home that I was asked to contribute a few lines for the house monthly newsletter, describing my job.

As I worked in the laundry, that was not going to be very interesting was it? I ended up writing a shortened version of the chapter headed 'All washed up'. It went so well I was asked to write some more and finished up doing more articles for them that were also well received.

Jane the homes 'activities lady' was the one who suggested I should write a book, so blame her not me.

I hope you enjoy this tongue in cheek look at my early years as much as I enjoyed writing it.

CHAPTERS

1 In the beginning

2 Earliest memories

3 School days

4 Sink or swim

5 Then there was three

6 Did somebody mention pudding

7 Golden shoes

8 The way it was

9 The beautiful rocking horse

10 Easter parade

11 All aboard

12 Can you come out to play?

13 Don't swing on the gate

14 Never did me no harm

15 It doesn't matter what it looks like

16 A trip to the dentist

17 All stuck up

18 All washed up

19 Anyone for Christmas cake

20 Christmas times past

21 Up the garden path

Chapter One

In the beginning

I was one year old when we moved into a brand new council house in a small village deep in the Essex countryside where Dad's parents lived, not that I can remember it of course. The year was 1951, the second world war was behind us and things were improving. Our family consisted of Dad, Mum, my big sister who was eighteen months older than me, and little me. My parents soon realised how lucky they were to have me as I was born with beautiful auburn hair and cried twenty-three out of twenty-four hours a day, every day. The one hour a day of peace was while I was getting my breath back. We had lived with Mum's parents until now in the neighbouring village, so imagine how upset they must have been watching us trundle down their path in our big black twin pram on our way to our new home. I bet they missed me

I loved our twin pram, my sister and I sat one each end looking fondly at each other, and if I may modestly say, we looked absolutely adorable, as many a grown-up would say as we passed. I quickly discovered that if I reached out while Mum wasn't looking, I could bash my sister on the nose and make her cry. Mum would then tell her off for crying for no reason and tell her that if she didn't stop she would get "something to cry about". She didn't, so Mum did. I never tired of that game.

Our new home was on a small brand new council estate of ten houses and six bungalows so we were all new together. The houses all had three bedrooms and families with young children moved into them. The bungalows were for the old folk, I'm allowed to say that because I'm one myself now. It seems strange to me now, but they built the bungalows between the houses full of young children and the school. Perhaps they thought all old people were deaf, but we discovered they could hear perfectly well when we didn't want them to. It was good because we children all grew up together and went through school together, although we were not always the best of friends, all of us going home with bumps and bruises from time to time.

Dad had finished his National Service by now, he had been a Petty Officer in the Navy and he now worked for a local firm in the small town five miles away which meant quite a bike ride for him every day
in all weathers. Mum knitted him a nice warm hat which he pulled down over his ears in the cold weather and with his roll-up cigarette stuck permanently to his lower lip and a pencil stuck behind his ear, he looked really handsome. In the summer he wore his woolly hat above his ears which meant he could keep a pencil behind one ear and a cigarette behind the other. He was very clever, our Dad, he could turn his hand to anything from building our childhood bikes to repairing everything. If Dad did something it was done properly and if he couldn't mend it no-one could.

Mum got the short straw and had to look after us girls and the house, no easy task in the days before vacuum cleaners and washing machines. I can still see her now in her wrap-around apron and her headscarf knotted at the front, as was the fashion then. She was always sweeping, dusting, polishing, cooking, washing and trying to keep us two in line. In the living room we had a carpet but either side of the Rayburn was a large gap between the carpet and the wall which Mum would polish red, the gap, not the wall. Occasionally I would help her with the polishing, but only occasionally, it was too much like hard work for me.

The house had three bedrooms, my sister and I having one each, but poor Mum and Dad had to share, and an upstairs bathroom.. Mum and Dad's bedroom had a fireplace in but the other rooms did not have any heating . Downstairs we had a living room, the only warm room in the house as it had the Rayburn. For those of you wondering what that is, it's the poor man's Aga. Just don't tell Aga owners I said that, they're a touchy bunch where their ovens are concerned. To put it simply a Rayburn has a fire, an oven, and a hotplate on the top where we always had a kettle on the boil, which is probably why I am the biggest tea drinker in the world, well in this street anyway.

At the back we had the kitchen / scullery. Do houses still have sculleries, you don't hear of them these days do you? We had a small fold up table in there and a couple of chairs, an electric oven, and some linoleum on the floor. Dad put some shelves up so Mum had somewhere to put her saucepans.
From the kitchen sink there was a nice view of the large vegetable garden, so she could keep an eye on Dad and make sure he wasn't leaning on his spade nattering to the man next door.

Just off the scullery we had a big walk in pantry, where I seemed to spend a lot of my time, possibly because not only do I like my tea I love biscuits, buy me a packet of biscuits and I'm your friend for life. There are only two types I don't like but I'm not going to tell you what they are because I just know they will be the ones you buy me if I tell you.

We did not have refrigerators in those days of course which meant we had to store things carefully somewhere cool, standing the cheese, milk and butter on the stone floor in the pantry and keeping the meat in a safe. The safe was made of wood with a small-holed grill on the front which would let air in but kept flies out, most of the time. Of course we didn't have sell by dates, if the food smelled off we didn't eat it and guess what? We survived and saved quite a bit of money. We've been in the pantry so long I think I better have another biscuit or two before we leave, standing in a Pantry is hungry work you know.

We had a front room which was only ever used for best. It had an open fire place and the best three piece suite in it. We girls were not allowed in this room unless accompanied by a responsible adult. It was the type of room that had the Queen come to visit she would have been taken there, but she didn't so it went unused. We were also the proud owners of an outside loo, passage and shed, but we spent most of our time in the living room, we had our family meals in there all sat around the dining table together, fancy that. We used to play in the living room in the cold weather as all the other rooms were too cold to stay in very long. The bedroom window panes would be frozen inside in the winter creating the most beautiful intricate patterns in the ice, each one was different. We girls got very good at getting dressed in bed under the covers ,probably not hygienic, but better than getting frostbite in the nether-regions.

While Mum worked really hard indoors Dad worked hard outside creating the gardens, we had a flower garden and lawn at the front bordered by a hedge which Dad shaped into turrets, and an enormous vegetable garden at the back. He planted fruit trees and bushes around the edges, laid the paths, put the washing lines up, built a chicken coup and our rabbit hutches for us. Over the fence at the very end of the vegetable garden was the farmer's field leading down to the river at the bottom.

Now I know this must seem ungrateful considering we all had brand new homes, but there was something not quite right with them. On our side of the road (it wasn't a proper road just pot holes and rubble at the time), all our front doors were on the side of the houses, while the houses opposite correctly had their front doors on the front, but their back doors were on the side. This was long before some bright spark came up with the idea of " taking your children to work week" therefore completely destroying everything you had achieved the previous year. I think what had happened was that the architect had taken the plans home one night and left them on the table while he read his newspaper and one of his children, instead of finishing his homework, had just doodled on the plans altering them slightly and when they were built no-one noticed until it was too late.

As I have mentioned before, the village was only small, with a mixture of old and new homes. Part of the village had been destroyed by fire years before, apparently by a young girl playing with matches in a barn of straw. Her parents couldn't send her to bed without her tea on this occasion as a punishment because that had burned down as well. I bet she wasn't very popular with the rest of the villagers that day. It was not me, I had not been born then, although it may have been possible in a previous life.

The church stands proudly in the centre of the village with it's striking clock which chimed every quarter of an hour day and night, very useful if you couldn't sleep and wanted to know the time. It's fair to say we were not regular Church goers in our family, I did join the Church choir however, but then the sun came out, the farmer cut the corn and there were straw bales to climb over, and as that appealed more to me I left after about three weeks. I can't sing anyway, so they may not have missed me too much. Mum said it was a High Church, but it wasn't up a hill or anything.

There was a small shop, the size of a small living room, in fact it was the living room, which sold everything you needed from hairgrips to hacksaws. They also sold pear drops, I love pear drops in case you were wondering. It was owned by a couple, he was a small Scot and she was a big Brit, need I say more? They were a very enterprising couple as on Monday afternoons the Doctors held their weekly surgery in another room in the house. They also ran the local taxi service, which was their car. Two public houses, one opposite the church and the other on the outskirts of the village provided nourishment for the grown ups and the occasional bag of crisps for us.

Our primary school, which was in the centre of the village, had three classrooms and a walled concrete playground. The headmistress lived in the house attached to the school with her father. He was a keen gardener and the garden was always immaculate. Right in the middle was an enormous mound of neatly trimmed turf which was hiding the Anderson shelter which he now used for storing school equipment. We used to use the gardens for special occasions like dancing around the maypole and practicing the high jump as the lawn was lovely and springy to land on. Across the road from the school was the recreational ground. It had three swings and a large slide plus a cricket pitch and pavilion. We used this for school sports like running or playing rounder's or when the boys played cricket during school time. The cricket pitch was used on Sundays by the village team to play against other local teams. We weren't bothered by traffic then as there were few cars around, we were more likely to get mown down by a pram or a bike while crossing the road. The recreation ground was also used for the annual fete, every August Bank Holiday, or as the signs still say, "Remember the date of our village fete, August Bank Holiday Monday." At the entrance to the recreation ground was the village hall, it had a nice large room with a stage at one end, very useful for the school plays and other social gatherings like weddings and funerals. It had a balcony upstairs, obviously, and a fair sized kitchen area complete with big tea urn, cups, saucers and plates. It served us well over the years and with a bit of modernization is still going well today.

We relied on delivery people then, the milkman called daily and, as he lived in the village if we needed an extra pint we would pop round to his house. He kept the milk in a brick outhouse which was nice and cold. We would pay him the money and then go and help ourselves to the milk. There was a grocery van that came round once a week as well as a butcher and of course the newspaper was delivered daily. Most of us grew our own vegetables, we had fruit as well, the local farm sold eggs, although we did have half a dozen bantams so we had fresh eggs daily.

We had a bus service daily taking us into the small market town five miles away. Well it was a sort of service. It left the village at 8.30am which got you into town by 9am so you could get to work, which was great, but it then left the town at 4pm so you couldn't get home from work, very useful. There was also a bus that run twice weekly in the afternoon, going through neighbouring villages in a big circle.

We were lucky, we had a dog, he used to run away frequently but came back when he was hungry, and at least two cats, mainly because the cat next door kept having kittens which we seemed to end up feeding, and pet rabbits and a couple of guinea pigs which we were expected to look after. Their hutches had to be cleaned out regularly, with the contents being wheeled in the wheelbarrow and emptied on the compost heap at the top of the garden, for some reason this always seemed to be my job. Dad made us wire runs so we could put the rabbits and guinea pigs out during the day to eat the grass.

Another of our jobs was to spend ages picking armfuls of dandelions and hog weed along the grass verges for the rabbits and guinea pigs to eat, which meant our hands were always covered in dandelion Stains. We had plenty of space to exercise the dog and play, including a large expanse of waste ground next to where our houses had been built. This ground was also useful for building a big village bonfire ready for firework night. I hate the sound of fireworks so I only ever watch them from indoors, in fact I'm a right misery on bonfire night, and several people will vouch for that. We were surrounded by fields which we used to play in, when the farmer wasn't looking of course. We would scour the hedges looking for bird's nests, we knew not to touch them though . We would peer in to see how many eggs or babies there were. We got to know the different eggs when we saw the discarded shells on the ground. We listened for the Cuckoo which was always in full voice in April, although to this day I have never managed to see one. We would peer down rabbit holes in the hope of seeing a furry bunny. We were taught to be curious but not to be cruel to the animals.

I think it is fair to say that all of us that moved into those houses were neither better or worse off than each other, we children certainly had all we needed, food in our tummies, fresh air in our lungs, fields to play in, and our imaginations. There was also plenty of work around for the grown-ups, if my memory serves me right all the Dad's went off to work, some worked on the land that surrounded us, some of them, like our Dad, had quite a journey to make as well, but no-one thought anything of it, it was simply how life was. I know one or two of the Dad's were fond of the pub, but our Dad was lucky, he didn't have to choose between home and pub, Mum made his decision for him. Mind you, we children did not have it all our own way, these were the days when "children should be seen and not heard", we were expected to "speak when we were spoken to", treat all adults with respect, and we never ever swore as you would be severely punished if you did. Grown up conversations were never discussed in front of us floppy-eared children, and at every meal you were reminded of the starving children in the world. I was obviously very soft hearted because I was quite happy for them to have my Brussels sprouts and liver and bacon every time, but they weren't getting my pudding. Oh no, that was mine and only mine.

That's me on the left, making sure the coast is clear!

Chapter 2

Earliest memories.

I think it is fair to say that I do not have too many pre- school memories but what I have I will share with you, I'm kind like that you know. I remember standing with my arm in a plaster cast screaming my head off. No, no-one was hurting me, I was just screaming for effect. I had apparently broken my left arm, and I know you'll be feeling sorry for me but your sympathy, along with Mum's, is probably going to be short lived. You see I did it when I fell off the dog. Yes, Mum had told me several times not to ride on the dog's back. He was a good natured Labrador cross. On this particular day though I think the cross bit got the better of him and he decided he'd had enough, so he unseated me and left me lying in a crumpled heap in the middle of the living room floor doing what I do best, screaming my head off. I was only two at the time so I'm pleading age as my defence. Anyway, there I am at out-patients at our local small hospital waiting to have the plaster checked, I've been waiting for ages, about ten minutes probably, and I'm bored. There are several other people plastered, so to speak, all awaiting their turn quietly, and one or two are looking sideways at me, probably thinking what a sweet little girl I look, which of course I was.

Out - patients consisted of a large room painted that shade of green that if you weren't feeling sick when you arrived you soon would be, and smelling strongly of ether. The sides were lined with chairs, and it had a high ceiling and an echo just waiting for a little person to try out, so I did. Despite Mum's best efforts to stop me I put on such a convincing display of distress and noise, with my cute little red crumpled tear lined face obviously bringing the caring side out in the nurses, that I was soon checked and shoved back out onto the street, and they didn't even give me a sweet for being good and brave. What upset me most about breaking my arm was that Mum said up until then I had been left handed and now I had to start all over again and train my right hand to punch my sister on the nose. I managed it though, it's surprising what you can do if you really want to. A few years later my sister broke her arm, but being older and wiser, she fell off a horse, the show off.

Despite my early introduction to hospital I have never been scared of them, in fact I think they are more scared of me. My second job after leaving school, strangely enough, was working in a large city hospital. Ok, they have knocked it down since. Actually they started while I was still there, but I'm sure that was only coincidence.

Apparently, and I know you won't believe this of me, I used to bite. It was only my big sister I used to bite, so that's not quite so bad is it? Poor Mum tried everything to stop me, from bribery to smacking me, but to no avail. I suppose that as I was about four by then these threats and treats were wearing off a bit. My sister didn't have spots, just teeth marks all over her. In desperation Mum caught hold of me just as I cornered my sister and was about to attack and bit me really hard, leaving an angry mark on my arm. I'm sure you are horrified at that aren't you? And I bet you're now on the 'phone to social services. Good job too, Mum felt really bad about it and carried the guilt for years so she certainly needed a sympathetic ear. She probably could have done with a few sessions of counselling to overcome the trauma of it all, especially as it was years later when she confessed to me what she'd done. Me? I don't remember it at all, but I never bit anyone again.

You know what it's like when you are told not to do something don't you? Me too.

Granddad had just concreted his path and carefully cordoned it off so no-one would tread on it, but someone did didn't they? I would have got away with it too if they hadn't spotted the wet concrete on my shoes. I was really lucky though, this Granddad, Mum's Dad, or Wim Granddad as we called him, absolutely adored me, a feeling that I returned in bucket loads. If you're walking up a path with little footprints in, be careful, they might be mine, because they are still there, Granddad never removed them. For those of you who have never met me and may be picturing me as a sweet little child with lovely shiny hair I feel I need to point out that that is not me, you are getting me muddled up with my sister. Yes of course I was a sweet little child, it's the shiny hair you have got wrong. My lovely auburn locks had vanished and had been replaced by brown curls. Before you get all misty eyed picturing lovely luxurious curls falling neatly into ringlets on my shoulders I can honestly say that my curls are nothing like that. My hair has the texture of wire wool and curls that stick out wherever you don't want them to. It doesn't grow long it grows outwards, and the mention of rain instantly transforms them into a ball of frizz. Not a pretty sight trust me. Whenever I went to the hairdressers to get a haircut people would comment on my "lovely curls". They did look lovely lying on the floor, I always thought that was the best place for them. Mum thought they were lovely, mainly because Dad's was the same, but he was lucky, he could slather them in grease to keep them in place. When I was about three and my sister four the fashion was to have a series of waves at one side of the parting and Mum being a fashionable sort of person decided we girls should have this style. She had discovered a special lotion called "Wavy bounce" or "Wave goodbye" or something like that. So there we sat, on the table, while she applied it. Once applied it needed to be held in place with clips until it "set", usually about a week. Dad came up with a brilliant idea for keeping it in place, bulldog clips. Unfortunately the only ones he had were industrial size and as we needed one per wave, by the time they were all applied they were so heavy that our heads were now resting on one shoulder. We were then allowed out to play with them in place, although we had a lopsided view of the world.

We soon discovered a problem with these clips, if you went past a magnet you would find your head clamped to it and it took a grown-up to rescue you. That was ok as long as you could find a grown-up, but what if you couldn't? You could be stuck there for a week. Luckily as there were only us two girls in the family Mum would notice if one of us was missing after a couple of days and come looking for us, but what if you came from a big family? You might not be missed for weeks, or if your Mum had so many children that she had lost count, you might not be missed at all. There may still be some children out there still attached to magnets, do you think we ought to go and check just in case?

Once our clips were removed Mum would study our new hairstyles carefully. My sister's looked really pretty with it's waves neatly in place, her shiny little face and big twinkling eyes gazing fondly up at Mum, and Mum's face would beam with delight. Mine, on the other hand would spring up as soon as released and although the waves were there, they stuck up on the top of my head like a staircase. All I got from Mum was "I don't know why I bothered." Me neither. Mind you that lotion was strong, I've still got the "stairs" now. We used to go to the hairdressers to have our hair "thinned out" and when the new trend came in for a "razor cut" Mum took us for that as well, it felt like they were sawing your hair off with a blunt razor, which by the end of the day they probably were. In desperation Mum decided to let my hair grow long to see if the curls would drop with the weight. They didn't, they just grew outwards and she had to spend ages extending the ribbons on my bonnet.

That's enough talk about my hair, I find it very depressing, so here's something better. As I have mentioned before Dad worked at a large local firm when we were small. His sister, Auntie En, and Mum's sister Auntie Dee. also worked there. Auntie En worked there for a long time, Auntie Dee and Dad for a shorter time. Still with me? Good. Every year this firm would host a massive Christmas party for all their employees' children, about two hundred people in total. I have found out recently that the money for the party was raised through fund raising by the Social Club at the firm. Auntie En was the treasurer of this club and she tells me they spent all year raising the money, buying all the presents and wrapping them, organised all the food and all the entertainment, so I would like to say on behalf of all us children that had a wonderful time, a great big thank you to all of you for all the hard work . We were all dressed in our best clothes and on our best behaviour, even me. The party was held in a massive hall, about the size of an aircraft hanger. We would sit at the massive tables to eat our tea, sandwiches, cakes, biscuits ,jelly and drink large amounts of orange squash. After tea the tables would be cleared and removed, the chairs put in rows and once we had all settled down the entertainment would start. We'd have jugglers, singers, musicians and people making animals out of balloons. I would love to know if these entertainers were some of the workers. It was wonderful and of course right at the end Father Christmas would appear with his sleigh and big sacks of presents. Each child had there own present with their name carefully written on it and when Father Christmas called your name you went up onto the stage to receive your present from the great man himself, Bliss. Do firms still do this today? It meant so much to us children, we all used to look forward to it.

Dad and Mum

Chapter three.

School days.

Our village primary school consisted of three classrooms and we had three female teachers. The headmistress taught the oldest children and like the others was a firm but fair lady. There were about seventy of us children divided into classrooms by age. We all knew each other pretty well by the time we were school age because most of us came from the village although there were a few who came by bus from the next village. Quite a few of us had brothers and sisters at school together, including me and my big sister of course.

In the winter we had fires in the classrooms to keep us warm, they were black metal ones which Nan, being the school caretaker, lit early in the morning. The playground was concrete and surrounded by a high red brick wall, to stop us escaping. The toilets were outside at the far side of the playground, I'm sure they put them as far away as possible to stop us from spending too much time in them in the winter.

Our day would start with assembly before we went into our separate classes. We used to recite our times table daily, you remember how it goes, once one is three, two threes are nine, seven nines are ninety four. We also had a weekly spelling test, I was good at spelling. I knew you would be surprised. I did say used to be, as in long ago. I can't possibly remember everything I learnt at school, there's only so much room in my little head. Well actually there's a lot of space but I'm saving it for something really important. During lessons we would hear the dinner van come with the big metal containers followed by a lot of clanging as they were unloaded and put in the big ovens to keep the food warm. At break time the milk monitor would bring our small bottle of milk and a straw to each of us to drink before we went outside to play. Sometimes if we were lucky we got orange juice instead of milk, perhaps the farmer couldn't be bothered to get up early that morning and milk the cows or something.

We had basic lessons in sewing, the girls not the boys. The headmistress would tell us stories while we sewed. One girl was listening so intently that when the lesson finished she had sewn her needlework to her dress. We also learnt cross stitch, always useful when making covers for cushions.. These practical lessons were great for people like me whose hands are much cleverer than their brains. Mum and Dad taught me to knit. Dad, being a Petty Officer in the Navy before we were born, probably spent a lot of time on a boat knitting fishing nets or something I should think.

We had P.E. also, balancing on beams, on the floor not the ceiling. Trying to jump over the horse, the teacher would give us a hand from behind and we would fly over it and land on our noses the other side. We would climb up the ropes and ignore the advice to climb down the parallel bars and slide down the rope instead, burning our hands and a big hole in the back of our shorts. Do you remember the rubber mats we had on the floor to do forward rolls and headstands on? If you were lucky you could kick somebody else while doing this, if you weren't lucky it was you that got kicked I enjoyed P.E. at primary school, it got rid of all that excess energy. For running and games we used the recreation ground. I was a good sprinter and also good at the high jump, it was scissor jumping then, none of this throwing yourself over backwards. The secret to being good at these sports is very simple, apart from a mother on the warpath, you just need long legs.

I represented our school at the school inter-sport competition each year. It was a huge event with all the local schools taking part and all the children packed into the stands screaming for their school. I usually came last in the sprint because I was too busy watching what was going on around me and forgot to listen out for the starting pistol. One year I did come tie third in the high jump but only because someone broke the cane and we had to use a rope instead that sagged in the middle, but at least I got a certificate, and only you and I know about the sagging rope.

Just when you think everything in life is sweet and perfect and the only thing you've got to worry about is how much custard to pour on your sponge pudding at lunch time something like this happens. We were sat in class copying from the blackboard when my sister put her hand up and said she couldn't see the writing on the board. She walked forward until she could see it clearly, as the Headmistress advised her, by which time she was level with the front row where I was sitting. Now, you would have thought that being the big sister, and "older and wiser" than me she would have realised that if she sat on the front row and squinted like I was, then she could have seen the writing on the board. But no. Mum took us both to get our eyes tested on the advice of the teacher and we both ended up with pink plastic national health glasses. Thanks Sis, I now had frizzy hair and pink plastic glasses alongside a growing epidemic of freckles. To think, I had been so lovely to her all those years and that's the thanks I got. That's the trouble with big sisters, just when you think you've got the upper hand, they go and do something horrible like ruining your whole life by making you wear glasses. If you have a big sister, watch her closely at all times, they cannot be trusted. I shall be watching mine closely from now on, especially now as I can actually see her with my new glasses.

One thing I have never figured out about our Primary school days was why the girls always wore brown shoes and the boys always wore black, do you know? It was the nearest we ever got to a uniform. Perhaps it was so that the teachers knew who were girls and who were boys, but as the girls wore dresses and the boys wore shorts , you would have thought that would have given them a clue. I do know we were never allowed to have our hair near our eyes, fringes had to be cut, and loose hair had to be clipped securely in place or plaited, so that you didn't strain your eyes. Not that mine ever grew in a fringe or loose in front of my face, in fact I should think my hair caused other people eye strain trying to see round it.

    I bet some of you can remember this, at 11am on a Friday morning we would be stood in our t- shirts, shorts and slip-on black pumps in the middle of the classroom, cleared of desks and chairs of course, waiting for the radio to be turned on. "Good morning children" the announcer would say and the music would start. One minute you had to be as tall as a tree, stretching your arms up as far as you could while balancing on tippy-toes, the next you were curled up tightly in a ball on the floor being a tiny mouse and gathering splinters in hard to reach places.. The music would change and you would be a ballet dancer pirouetting around the floor, or a red Indian doing a rain dance around a camp fire. In most of our cases you couldn't tell the difference. I think our school must have had firm foundations. We would then drag our rubber mats onto the floor, lie on our backs and cycle in the air, followed by forward rolls and sometimes even handstands. I don't know about you but all that exercise has made me hungry. I'm ready for dinner now, after we've put all the desks and chairs back of course and got changed. We would form an orderly queue with our plates waiting our turn to be served. Of course one of our dinner ladies was our Nan, but I still had to have Brussels sprouts, which I thought was a bit cruel. Mind you, I was always first in the queue for pudding , especially sponge pudding with lashings of custard, or jelly with a big dollop of ice-cream or sometimes evaporated milk, yummy. Why was it called evaporated milk when it clearly hadn't because it was still in the tin? I am by nature a slow eater, I inherited that from my Dad, and often used to miss playtime because I was struggling to eat my food. In my defence I will add it wasn't because I was a chatterbox, in fact at pudding time you couldn't even get a grunt out of me. Of course I could have gone without pudding, but given the choice I would rather go without playtime.

    We also did country dancing, lining up in the playground opposite our partners waiting for the gramophone to be wound up. Once the music started we would grab our partners crossed outstretched hands and swing as fast as possible through the line, hoping that we were still on our feet by the end. When we reached the end we waited to see if the next pair could do it any faster. Elegant we weren't, but we were enthusiastic. My dance partner was always the same lad, we always sat on the same table for our lessons as well and whenever I needed a partner for anything he was always it. I bet he was glad to leave primary school, in fact I bet he was first out the gate poor lad. He did threaten to hit someone on the head with the cricket mallet one day, only joking of course, but unfortunately as he swung the mallet the head flew off and smashed one of the big classroom windows. Perhaps he wasn't so bad after all.

    Who remembers sums at school? I quite liked them but those triangles baffled me. I quite liked iced- sausage triangles, but I wasn't so keen on the highpotofmousse ones. Do you remember the questions we had to answer in our maths lessons? Things like……….Johnny had nineteen sweets, six soft centres and thirteen hard. Bridget only liked hard centres but Andrew liked only soft ones. Harriet liked both. How did Johnny share them out so they all got the ones they liked and they all had an equal share? How the hell would I know? Johnny should have kept quiet about them and ate them all himself, I would have.

We used to spend ages writing stories at school, do you remember the books? They had lines on the bottom half for the words and a big blank space at the top for your drawing. I loved getting a new book, the first page was always done in your best handwriting, but by the second page you were back to scrawl and big ink blots weren't you?

We had quite a few musical lesson as well, whether it was singing while one of our teachers played the piano, or playing with all the different instruments we had in the cupboard. I usually ended up with the triangle but by the time it got round to my one and only ting I had got fed up and was busy looking out the window and completely missed my cue. Several of us did learn to read music and play the recorder so that when we put on a play we always had our own orchestra. I've just had a thought, I cannot sing, just ask anyone who knows me, they will tell you that's true, so maybe that's why we were encouraged to play instruments that we needed to blow into. Teachers aren't daft are they? Perhaps that's why orchestra's are so large, they are full of all the people who can't sing. I think my favourite lesson was on a Friday afternoon when our teacher would read us a story and we would sit quietly listening, well apart from the snoring of course, but we were good children, we let the teacher sleep. On really hot summer days we would take our books across the road to the recreation ground and sit in the shade of a big tree and read quietly, the only sounds to be heard being the birds singing, the bees buzzing around and the very occasional sound of a car travelling along the main road.

    I can remember going on holiday with the school to the seaside one year. It must have been the top two years that went because I can remember my sister was there as well. Two of our teachers accompanied us, we must have gone on a coach which must have taken a good couple of hours to get there. We slept in huts, the girls in one and the boys next door. The boys got into serious trouble one day because they jumped into our hut through the window at the back and leaped out through the window at the front, right in front of the teachers. We had bunk beds which were great fun, especially if you got a top bunk.. The holiday camp was right on the seafront, the only thing separating us from the sea was a vast expanse of grass, the size of several football pitches, followed by a steep drop down the cliffs. Our teachers took us down the steep craggy path to the sea on one occasion. We had a big lecture beforehand about being really careful and walking slowly at all times as it was quite dangerous. Some smart Alec thought they knew better didn't they? I ended up at the bottom on my back having grazed most bits of me as I tumbled down and knocking a few of the others over on the way. Popular I was not. There was a big indoor games room where we could play table tennis, snooker or board games or cards, or simply sit and talk. At bedtime we would try and frighten each other with ghost stories. Not that I was any good at them, they scare me too much. It was our first taste of freedom, it was brilliant.

    One of my most vivid memories of that holiday was seeing a big petrol lawn mower coming towards us seemingly on it's own. As it got closer we realized there was someone controlling it, he was a dwarf, it's probably not PC to say that now but it was then. Having never met a dwarf before we were fascinated by him. He lived close by with his family, who he took us to meet. His children were naturally very protective of their Dad and a bit wary of us to start with, but as the week went on they realised we adored their Dad as much as they did. He worked so hard at that camp, on the go the whole time. We all came away with the fondest memories of him, his wife and his family, memories I still hold today.

I know you will be impressed by this. I was once the May Queen at school. Had I been extra good that year? No. Was I the teacher's pet? Hardly. Had I eaten all my Brussels sprouts that time, what do you think? No, I was the one who had a white Bridesmaid dress with pretty red rosebuds on it that I had worn when Auntie En got married a few weeks before, so I got the part. I had a cane with a ribbon tied on the end, which I found really useful for prodding people in the back, and all I had to do was sit on my throne and look pretty. I was, if I say so myself, perfect for the part. All the Mums were invited, it was a lovely sunny morning and everyone was sat on the headmistress's lawn waiting for the maypole dancing to start. We had practised until we were perfect with our ribbons, in and out in time to the music, leaving pretty patterns on the pole as we went. The record player was wound up, the music started and off we skipped. We were going down a storm until one girl spotted her Mum in the audience and stopped to wave to her. The resulting mayhem saw us all wrapped up in each other's ribbons, dodging from side to side saying "no, it's my turn to go over not yours", until the teacher stopped the music and grabbed the wobbling pole to top it from falling over. Many of the girls were in tears and ran to be comforted by their Mums, leaving the teachers to unravel the ribbons. Eventually the ribbons were untied and the infant, who had wandered across the lawn as the dance had started, was released after spending the entire time bound to the pole. He was ok and came back to school the next week. All in all another successful performance.

I guess what we were aiming for at school was passing the 11 plus, that all important exam that decided which school you went to next. I know you will be shocked to know that I failed mine, but did I care? Of course not, I didn't want to go to another school at all.

There's one last thing you need to do before you leave if you will be so kind, put your chairs quietly on top of your desk ready for the school cleaner. You've got it, our Nan. Thank you.

School days don't come better than that. Yes we were lucky living where we did, but have you any idea where I went to school? I'm leaving you little clues in this book. Hope you find my village.

Me and sis in second row on our school holiday

Chapter four

Sink or swim.

Once a week while we were at primary school we would be taken to the local swimming baths in the market town 5 miles away for a lesson. We used to go in the same mini bus that delivered our lunch to school. All the heavy metal containers would be taken out and put in the kitchen and we would all pile in. It was an old mini bus, the ones that had a long seat down each side and were really slippery, so if the driver braked you would all slide along the seat.

I looked forward to going to the swimming baths but hated our swimming lessons. No it doesn't make sense to me either, perhaps I just liked the journey in the mini bus and blanked out the fact that once we arrived at the pool everything I hated most would be there. I couldn't swim, I didn't like the cold water, I didn't like the echo that all swimming pools seem to have and I couldn't put my rubber swimming hat on properly either. No matter how I tried my hair always stuck out the back of the hat while the front was so far forward that I had such big frown lines on my forehead that I couldn't see where I was going. As the hat covered my ears I couldn't hear either so everything sounded muffled. Once in the pool I would cling onto the side shivering while the instructors tried to persuade me to let go of the rail and try using a float. I'm sure you can remember them, they were white, square and made out of something like polystyrene which made them very light. I found they didn't float with me, they just shot out of my grasp and after giving me a nasty clunk on the nose would leave me flailing about in the water until I sank. I did not like going under the water, mainly because that would be the exact same time that I decided to take a deep breath in. My lungs, like various other parts of me, do not like water. To make matters worse a lot of the other children in our school would be able to swim and splashed you every time they went by, on purpose I'm sure. My eyes don't like water either. I hope I don't come back as a fish.

Out of desperation the instructors took those of us that were not making any progress and taught us the breast stroke by letting us lie face down on a bench at the side of the pool and practice the strokes. I was really good at the strokes and had all the grace of a frog, a cold blue frog with a heavily lined forehead and in serious need of a good haircut I admit, but had I been allowed to take the bench with me into the swimming pool I would have been fine, but they wouldn't let me so I would simply flail around in panic, swallow gallons of water and sink to the bottom.

After several weeks of trying to teach us to swim without success, they decided that drastic action was needed. Did you know that if you point your hands up when you are under the water then you automatically rise to the surface? No I didn't either until the instructor explained that to me. Having nodded that we understood this, we were then pushed in the deep end by the instructors. It may seem a silly time to mention this, but when you've just been pushed in the deep end, and you are slowly sinking to the bottom in a muffled glug, glug, glug kind of way, and having swallowed loads of water because in the panic you open your mouth and inhale, the last thing on your mind is pointing your hands up.

I will give them credit though, if we hadn't surfaced by the end of the lesson they would get the big fishing net out and scoop us up off the bottom. They always counted us as we got back on the bus as well, just to make sure they hadn't missed any of us. It wouldn't do their reputation any good if half the class was still sat on the bottom of the pool when the next load of victims arrived would it?   Happily I did eventually learn to swim, anything to stop being pushed in the deep end. I got a certificate for swimming a width plus a sixpence from the school, which we all did when we had learnt to swim a width. If you don't know what a sixpence is, go and ask Grandma, she does. What still puzzles me though, is why can't you ever get properly dried after swimming and so you end up tugging your clothes on to a damp cold body? Also why were the changing rooms so small? Every time I bent down the doors would burst open and my bare bottom would be on full display to the entire school, or was that just me?

Chapter 5

Then there was three

Our Mum was feeling poorly so my sister and I had to go and stay with Rad Nan and Rad Granddad in the village for a while. They lived in the older council houses opposite The Red Lion pub. Auntie Dee came to look after Mum, and Dad and Auntie would call in and see us every day, probably to make sure we were behaving ourselves, which we were of course.

Although we were concerned about Mum we were reassured that she would be alright with a few days rest and we were happy staying with Nan and Granddad. They had a large garden, the front was mainly flowers with lawns, there was an enormous apple tree at the side of the house which we used to climb. We didn't eat the apples though, they were cooking apples and sour, although lovely once cooked in a pie with custard.

At the back of the house alongside the path they had a long vegetable garden. Every summer Nan would plant a big row of sweet peas in the middle, not only did they look pretty they smelled beautiful as well. Sweet peas always remind me of my Rad Nan and Granddad, and I always have some in my garden.

Nan and Granddad didn't mind what we got up to really as long as didn't do any damage. Granddad had two ferrets that he kept in hutches by the vegetable garden. They always seemed to be watching us with their beady looking eyes. Granddad loved his ferrets, but I was never very keen on them so I would give them a wide berth.

One of our favourite games was snail racing. We would hunt out two suitable snails, or Hoddydodds as we called them, from amongst Nan's plants and take them round to the front door. We would set them at the bottom in a line and then we would sit on the doorstep and watch them climb up the door. Mind you, they never went straight up so we had to keep a careful eye on them and correct them when they went off course. It used to keep us amused for hours, even if it did leave slimy trails on the door. If Nan called us in for lunch we would leave them where they were in the hope that they were still there when we had finished. We usually found that they had completely disappeared by the time we got back, it's surprising how quickly they can move when you don't want them to. We had to find two more and start again.

After a few days Dad came with the good news that Mum was feeling better and that we could go home. We packed our things and walked home with Dad glad to know Mum was better and we were looking forward to seeing her. When we walked in the house though Auntie told us to be quiet as Mum was very tired and sleeping upstairs, so we went and sat very quietly in the living room.

As we sat there we heard a tiny cry, and then it got louder and louder and we realised it was a baby crying. It was such a surprise, we didn't even know she had ordered one. We leapt up and started jumping up and down with excitement saying "we've got a baby, we've got a baby". Auntie then took us upstairs to meet our new baby sister, who cried a lot, but probably nowhere near as much as I had when I was a baby.

Over the next few days the discussions started as to what to call her. Mum and Auntie were determined that whatever name she had it couldn't be shortened. They had tried with our names without success so they weren't going to give in this time. Several days later they agreed on a name that it is true to say cannot be shortened, and pleased with themselves off they all went to register her. She now has a Birth Certificate with her name on, the only trouble is, none of us other than Mum and Auntie, have ever called her by it.

I have no idea how the name my other sister and I call her came about, it's not really a proper name at all. Add to that all her nieces and nephews call her something different to us, so very often we'll be talking about her using two different names in the same sentence. It's very confusing to anyone listening. I discovered she was known by another name at work when I 'phoned up to speak to her one day and they hadn't heard of her. To top it all though Dad always called her Sue, it isn't her name, it's nothing like her name, but that is what he always called her, no-one else ever called her Sue. I have a sneaking suspicion that Dad had wanted her to be called Sue all along but was out-voted.

After the initial excitement of having a new sister had subsided a bit, it began to dawn on me the difference it would make. When my Auntie asked me a few days later what I thought of my new sister, I burst into tears. I had wanted a horse, why couldn't Mum had had a horse?

The really strange thing is that she is the most sensible one amongst us, just don't tell her I said that. We didn't give her an easy time though. My big sister and I who were 8 and 7 when she was born, each had a dolls pram for Christmas that year and as our little sister was only a few weeks old she fitted in them nicely. We asked Mum if we could take her in one of our prams to visit Rad Nan and Granddad. It wasn't very far, just past the last bungalow, which was clearly visible from our house, and along the footpath across the field which led to their gate.. Mum was probably looking forward to the peace and quiet so she agreed as long as we did not let go of the handle, because she might fall out, the baby, not Mum. We promised to hold onto it tightly so she carefully wrapped her up and snuggled her down cosily and off we went. We both held the handle and we trundled along with the baby sleeping blissfully under her blankets. When we got past the last bungalow, which always had a stunning display of Dahlias in the garden, we turned into the field and out of sight of our house. We looked at each other , both obviously wondering if Mum had been right about her falling out of the pram. We both let go of the handle at the same time, and guess what? Mum was right, the pram tipped up and our sleeping sister fell head first into the field. We picked her up, dusted her down, and tucked her back in the pram and continued on our journey. It was several years later before we owned up.

Val Davina and me

Chapter six.

Did somebody mention pudding?

These days we are bombarded with information about what to eat, what's good for us and what isn't, on a daily basis. We had a much better system, we ate what was put in front of us.

Our Mum was a good cook and preparing our meals took up a large part of her day. Breakfast was usually porridge or cereals but if we ran out of these we would have bread and milk, white bread with warm milk and a covering of sugar. I loved that. Porridge of course was cooked in a saucepan on top of the Rayburn and had to be stirred all the time until it was ready. I can remember when I used to call for the girl who lived opposite to go to school, they were always running late and I would always end up stirring the porridge while her Mum plaited her hair. On Sundays Dad would often boil us girls an egg and cut us some soldiers to dip in the yolk. On one occasion he boiled an egg for our little sister but it exploded in the pan, I don't think she eats boiled eggs anymore. My big sister once asked Dad to boil her an egg and then changed her mind when he had. She ate her egg.

On school days we had a cooked lunch at school, anything from shepherds pie to beef stew, followed by my favourite of course, pudding with custard, cream, ice-cream or evaporated milk. Rice pudding, semolina, tapioca, I didn't care. I still dream of chocolate pudding with pink custard, can I have some please?

During the school holidays we used to have jam, peanut butter, banana or, if Mum wasn't looking, sugar sandwiches for lunch followed by a piece of homemade Victoria sponge filled with butter cream filling or jam, yummy.

Our tea in the school holidays would be a cooked meal which we all ate together when Dad got home from work. Mum would make us stews with dumplings, meat pies, pork chops, macaroni cheese, cottage pies, liver and bacon and our favourite, bacon, sausages, fried egg ,fried bread and baked beans. Sunday lunch was always a roast, chicken, beef, lamb or pork with Mum's home made Yorkshire pudding beaten within an inch of it's life. The chickens of course had to be plucked as they came complete with heads and feathers. I tried to miss that bit. As I've already mentioned Dad grew our vegetables so we always had a plentiful supply of parsnips, Swede, potatoes, carrots, peas, broad beans, runner beans, onions, beetroot, and these which I will whisper, cabbages, broccoli, spring greens and Brussels sprouts. I was not allowed to pick the Brussels sprouts because I could only ever find four, one for Dad, one for Mum and one for each for my sisters.   It was our job to peel the potatoes and prepare the vegetables each morning before going either to school or out to play. We used to have new potatoes and peas early in the year which Dad would pick and as he handed them to us always said "Don't eat the peas before dinner". It couldn't be done, we had to eat them as we removed them from the pods. Even now I cannot pass a row of peas without eating a handful. I also love eating raw potatoes, Mum said that when she was expecting me she used to crave raw potatoes and biscuits. See, I knew it wasn't my fault.

When we had lamb for dinner Dad would pick some fresh mint out of the garden and chop it into very fine pieces and then mix it with vinegar and sugar. The smell of mint sauce always makes my mouth water and takes me back to those times. Mum always put a sprig of mint in with the potatoes and peas. All our vegetables were cooked with a liberal sprinkling of salt. To preserve our vegetables in the days before fridges we used to store them in layers of salt in airtight jars. We would slice the runner beans and layer them between salt until the jar was full to the top before screwing the lid on and storing them in the pantry. This way our vegetables would last for weeks. We used to pickle the onions and red cabbage and beetroot so we would have a supply of them throughout the year. Mum and Dad also used to make some weird and wonderful wines, goodness knows what they tasted like, we children were not allowed to try them.

    Things like plums, gooseberries and greengages also got stored in jars, apples were kept in a cool dark place. Nan used to keep the cooking apples in her shed covered with straw, they had to be checked regularly because you know what they say about one bad apple, it is true. Between us and our grandparents we had a good supply of fruit in the gardens. As well as apples, plums, greengages, blackcurrants, rhubarb, strawberries and gooseberries there was also a plentiful supply of blackberries in the hedgerows along the lanes and fields of the village. We had bantams for fresh eggs and Wim Nan and Wim Granddad kept chickens as well so there were plenty of eggs to go round. Mum used to make the custard to go with our puddings and sometimes I was allowed to watch the milk come to the boil. It's fascinating watching the milk start to bubble and rise, so fascinating I would be so busy watching it that I would forget to remove it from the heat and it would boil over and burn. Burnt milk is not the nicest smell is it? We got quite used to it in our house though. Sometimes we would save the cream from the top of the bottle of milk and pour that over our pudding, if the Blue Tits hadn't got to the milk bottle first of course. We had the silver topped milk, which wasn't as creamy as the gold top which used to have about an inch of rich cream settled on the top. Grandma will tell you what an inch is, she knows everything. You could also get sterilized milk, which we didn't have, but the girl over the road did so I would make friends with her so that she would let me drink it, it was lovely. We also had evaporated and condensed milk in tins which kept a long time.

Now for my favourite bit, puddings. I shall be dribbling by the time I've written this. Mum would makes us fruit crumbles, fruit pies, jellies and trifles, rice puddings, sponge puddings and suet puddings. We always had a pudding after our main meal which in my case was the only way to get me to eat my main meal. Mum's sponge puddings were light and fluffy, they would either have homemade jam or fruit, or on really good days golden syrup in them. She used to make the sponge pudding, put it in a basin in a saucepan of water and leave it to boil for several hours. She also used to make a mean suet pudding. She would put it in a muslin cloth and tie the top tightly so it didn't escape, and leave that to boil in a saucepan of water. We used to eat it with our liver and bacon, covered in gravy. I didn't like liver and bacon but I had to eat it because of the suet pudding. She wasn't daft, our Mum. Now those of you that are already tut-tutting about my calorie intake had better skip the next paragraph altogether.

Mum would make a wonderful apple pudding with suet pastry. She would line the basin with the pastry, fill it with cooking apples and add spoonfuls of brown sugar before putting a pastry top on in, tying it up and putting it in a saucepan of water to boil. It's just as well we had the Rayburn to cook on. Any suet pudding that we didn't have with our liver and bacon Mum would serve up for pudding, smothered with golden syrup, the pudding, not Mum, so we got a double dose. I loved my Mum best of all on those days. As you know, pastry is very difficult to get right. My Nan made the best pastry I have ever tasted, she had been in service when she was a young girl and was taught how to make it properly. Her pastry would just melt in your mouth, I've not tasted anything to compare with it since. Alas I did not inherit this skill, my pastry comes with it's own health warning. Anyone attempting to cut my pastry needs to be very careful as it shoots off the plate and can seriously injure someone.

I think my Wim Granddad had the right idea about puddings. He always ate his pudding before his main meal. After he had eaten his pudding his main meal was served on the same plate, it didn't get washed in between. He also used to tip his cup of tea into his saucer to drink it. It didn't matter to me, he was my hero, he could do what he liked. Why wasn't I allowed to do the same thing? Just for any young readers who may be thinking what a simple life we had, we didn't have it all our own way you know. When we went to Nan and Granddad's, our Mum's parents, for a meal as children we were not allowed to speak at the table at all. If we went for Sunday tea to their house Nan always made a milk jelly and a fruit cake. My sister did not like milk jelly and I didn't like fruit cake but we weren't allowed to say anything so we had to eat them. We had to put our own salt on our crisps, yes, we had to unwrap the little blue bag of salt inside the packet and sprinkle it on. Our chewing gum came in a hard sugar coating that had different coloured layers, that you had to suck for hours to get to the gum. They were called gob stoppers, because they were so big they stopped you talking. They came in a machine which you had to put a penny in to release one. By the time you had got to the chewing gum it was time to go in for tea, so you had to put it in the rubbish bin. We used to have to drink out of glasses , the only exception being if we had a straw with a bottle of drink. We were not allowed to walk around with a drink, we always had to sit down. We were never allowed to eat in the street."Only common people ate in the street". Oh and ready meals ? Yes, that's when Mum used to open the door and shout "your dinner's on the table". You may think that with our calorie intake we were all overweight but we weren't. If we wanted to go anywhere we had to walk, run or bike. We were always outside playing when the weather was good, we spent very little time sitting indoors. We burned up all those calories with the exercise we got, plus we didn't get to eat many chips at all.

My sisters and me with Major the dog and my Granddad my hero

Chapter seven.

Golden shoes.

Just before the start of the school year Mum would take us to buy our new school shoes. We only had one decent shoe shop in town and by the time we got there the assistant was looking a bit frazzled. Mum always insisted we had a "good" brand of shoe so that our feet could grow properly so of course we used to have them measured. The measure, as some of you will remember, was a wooden ruler with a wooden slide that the assistant would slide to the tops of your toes to gauge the length of your foot and a tape measure that went around the width of your foot giving you the width you required. Still with me? Good. The wooden ruler can hurt if slammed against your toes, but I'm sure it wasn't deliberate, she must have been distracted or something, on this occasion. After measuring my feet the assistant announced with a groan "You've got odd feet". I wasn't having that, so I insisted they were not odd, they were the only ones I had. She shuffled off out to the back of the shop to find some shoes for me to try on.

I think she must have gone out for a tea break or a cigarette, or even a lie down, because she's taking a long time. Never mind, I'll give you a bit more information while we're waiting. It's lucky I was here to keep you amused really wasn't it? I don't want you dozing off now do I?

In time technology improved and the shoe shop installed a state-of-the-art x-ray machine. You placed your feet in the holes at the base of the machine and peered through the view finder to see…..your feet. This wasn't very exciting to me as I'd seen my feet earlier that day, Mum being Mum, had made me wash them in the wash basin that very morning. Oh how I wish I could still do that without the risk of pulling the basin off of the wall or having to call the fire brigade. You can just imagine that 999 call can't you? "Old lady with her foot stuck in the wash basin again, how many fire engines shall we send this time?". Just a brief glimpse into things to come, but she's on her way back now, and just as I thought, she's got biscuit crumbs around her mouth, but I'm not telling her.

        She's got four pairs of shoes in her arms all brown lace up ones with different designs on. She puts them down, explaining to Mum as she does that they are the only ones she can find that might fit someone with such odd feet as me. I'm sure she didn't have to say it that loud, everyone in the shop turned to see who she was talking about. I put my "butter wouldn't melt" face on, but they weren't impressed.

      I saw them instantly, sitting there in a shaft of sunlight, a pair of shoes that a princess would have worn, if a princess had to wear brown lace up shoes of course. My little eyes were transfixed on the pair of "golden shoes". It was love at first sight. Yes, I do fall in love with the strangest things, shoes, puddings, snails, spiders, you name it, I'm hooked on it. The assistant picked them up, dangled them under my nose, and smiled as she said, "Of course these aren't your size, but I brought them for you to try on anyway as you have such limited choice, having odd feet".

   I took them from her, yanked up my thick brown woolly socks as far as I could and rammed my feet into them. I tried so hard to convince Mum that they weren't pinching my toes or rubbing my heels and that the bulge by my toes was only my socks all bunched up, and not my toes at all. I even managed to do a convincing walk in them, or so I thought. Mum was having none of it though and made me take them off despite me pleading with her with my bestest tearful little face that my world would end if I couldn't have them. I slowly took them off and made a face at her behind her back, only to discover she was watching my reflection in the mirror opposite. Even my very best heartbroken look fell on stony ground again.

I had to try the other pairs of shoes on now starting with the awful ones, fortunately they were too narrow. The next pair, the ugly ones, were too tight and pinched my toes so that only left the hideous ones to try on. They were the biggest, heaviest, ugliest shoes I had ever seen. No one in their right mind would want to wear them. I put them on and winced, look they were far too short, my toes were crammed right up to the end. The assistant pressed the end of the shoe with her finger and it left an indentation between my toe and the end of the shoe. Next I tried the "they're squeezing my foot" trick, plenty of room to move she indicated. "Ouch they are rubbing my heels", she put a finger between my heel and the end of the shoe. She's really beginning to annoy me now.

Only the walk test left now, I needed to make that convincing. I limped, I winced, I whinged, I groaned as I took a few steps before declaring that they were agony and I couldn't possibly walk another step in them. My heels were bleeding I was sure, my toes were all scrunched up and turning blue I was convinced, and if Mum made me wear them my poor little feet would be permanently damaged. I cried as they insisted I walk the length of the shop in them, my sobs getting louder with each step, tears streaming down my face. I fell on the carpet and rolled in agony clutching my foot. I struggled to my feet again and limped my biggest limp back towards Mum. I sat beside her groaning and rubbing my feet for all I was worth to make her realise the agony I was going through. All to no avail. Better try plan B, I put my best sweet little daughter, "butter wouldn't melt" look back on. I bet you're feeling really sorry for me now aren't you? Mum turned to the assistant and said, "We'll take them, thank you". My "butter wouldn't melt" look vanished instantly, to be replaced with the ugliest, angriest face I could manage, and I can manage a few, and I stood with my hands on my hips scowling at my Mum. She turned to me and said " If the wind changes you will be stuck like that forever", turned around and went off to pay for the shoes.

As the new school term started and I walked into school in my horrible new shoes, convinced everyone was laughing at them, who should I see standing by the teacher's desk but little miss goody two shoes, the teacher's pet, who I never ever liked, and she was wearing my golden shoes. She had the biggest smile on her face and was busy showing off her new shoes to all her friends, who were all admiring them.. Life can be so cruel.

Me in my new shoes, plotting revenge

Chapter eight..

The way it was.

Now I know this will impress you, we had a telephone. Mind you we had to share it with the rest of the village. It sat in a red telephone box in the centre of the village right next to the church and the bus shelter. Why are they called bus shelters? They aren't big enough to get a bus in, although I bet a few drivers have tried, especially our school bus drivers.

When you made a 'phone call it cost you four pennies, proper pennies not those tiddly little things that get stuck in the corners of your purse. If I remember rightly, and I probably don't so I don't mind you correcting me, you put your money in and then dialled the number. When the person answered you pressed button A. If there was no answer then you pressed button B and got your money back.

Of course the only people who had telephones then were people like the doctor, the dentist and the vet. If we wanted to 'phone a friend in another village then we had to arrange a day and time beforehand so that they were waiting outside their phone box when we rang. What usually happened was that they would forget to be there, and when you rang it would be answered by someone slightly cross because they were waiting for a 'phone call from someone else. Of course you would also be cross because you had pressed button A and lost your money. The amazing thing was that most of the time we managed to say everything we needed to say to our friends when we saw them at school, so 'phoning them was only done for fun.

If Mum and Dad said "It's a lovely day today, lets go for a ride ", it didn't mean jumping in the car and going to the zoo or seaside. We got our bikes out and went for a bike ride. We would often cycle to the next village to see our Grandparents, it was a nice journey because we could go one way and then return another way. One way had a big hill down and then a big hill up straight after it and coming home the other way was slightly longer with a big hill down and a slightly smaller hill up past the church.

Dad had a baby seat on the front of his bike which our little sister used to sit on. Wim Nan and Granddad would always make a big fuss of us and if Auntie D. was there she would take us on the swings on their recreation ground which was right at the bottom of their garden. About three doors away from Nan and Granddad's house lived another of Mum's sisters, Auntie El. with our two cousins, so we would pop in and say hello to them.

If we were lucky Dad would stop outside the Red Lion on the way home and we girls would sit outside with a bottle of ginger beer and a packet of crisps each. Of course we were not allowed in the bar at all but we didn't mind we were more than happy to be grown up enough to sit outside in the sunshine. The ginger beer bottles were cold brown stone ones, we had straws of course, and plain crisps with the little blue bag of salt inside. Bliss.

Most Sundays we would go for a walk through the fields with Mum and Dad, it seemed like miles when we were little. We would see rabbits and birds, we would look for blackberries or hazelnuts, occasionally we would see a duck swimming in the river and if we had our Wellington boots on we would turn the stones over carefully in the river to see if there were any sticklebacks hiding underneath. Dad would throw sticks for the dog to catch or lift us up so we could see inside a bird's nest. We knew never to touch their eggs, and we learnt to respect all the creatures and birds. We would look at the ponies or the two donkeys grazing in their field.

Can you remember chilblains? We always used to be suffering from them. They would drive us crazy and we were forever scratching our toes, which as you know only made them worse. Mum used to smother our toes with Calamine lotion, that was good on sunburn as well. What about boils? We used to get those a lot, and sties on our eyes, usually on the very day the school photographer arrived, as if my photographs weren't bad enough already.

This one will bring tears to you eyes, Iodine. Do you remember when you would come in crying because you had fallen over and grazed your knee? First the graze would be carefully cleaned to remove any dirt or grit. That hurt didn't it? Next "the bottle" would appear, a harmless looking small brown bottle full of liquid that when applied to the skin turned it a yellowy brown. One single drop of this liquid when applied to your poorly knee would have you screaming at the top of your voice and it would take several grown-ups to peel you off the ceiling. You thought you were in pain before? Now you know what real pain is. Our Mum had a lot of faith in Iodine and slapped it on at every given opportunity believing it killed all known germs, the fact it almost killed her daughters was obviously a price worth paying in her eyes. Once you were done you were allowed back out to play with a big yellow stain on your knee, because the surrounding unbroken skin had received a good dollop as well, and the colour lasted for weeks. The thing is, you went back out to play feeling a lot worse than when you went in. If we ran out of Iodine in our house it was like the world had ended. Perhaps our Mum had shares in it or something.

Fancy a day off school snuggled up on the sofa under a blanket watching the telly while your Mum waits on you hand and foot? No chance. If we were ill enough to be off school then we were in bed, in a cold bedroom with the windows open so we could " get some fresh air" and "blow all the germs away". It was just you and your hot water bottle against the elements. If we had a cough we would get a dose of revolting cough medicine, just to make you feel worse. If you weren't eating then Mum would appear with a glass of warm milk with a raw egg mixed in it to "to build your strength up". Oddly enough, I quite liked that. I'll tell you what, we had to be pretty healthy to be ill then, and we got better very quickly.

This will have you in stitches, well hopefully not, but if you are I hear Iodine is good for them. Do you know what we used to do if we needed to see a doctor? We would go to the surgery and sit in the waiting room and wait. We didn't have appointments then, we knew the surgery would be open in the morning and again in the evening so we just used to turn up when we were ill. The doctors would see us all in turn and not leave until they had seen their last patient. Of course our doctors then had known all our families and watched us grow up. If we needed a doctor at night then our family doctor, or another doctor from the surgery would come after someone had sprinted into the village centre to call him from the 'phone box. Doctor's then used to work days and nights so if they had to make a home visit you knew the doctor that was "called out" would be familiar to you, and he would know you as well. Of course we weren't lucky enough to have the foresight to know that we were going to be ill in two weeks time like you do now. That's progress I suppose. Doctors used to hold surgeries in the villages on different days for the people who couldn't get into town. They may not have been as private as today's surgeries, some were held in the village halls or someone's spare room in their house, but it didn't matter as we all discussed out ailments while we were waiting anyway, and some of the remedies were better than the doctor's. Iodine came top of the list, followed closely by calamine lotion.

I can remember when we had the smallpox scare. We all had to go and be vaccinated. We all went to one of the village surgeries. There were masses of people there. I thought somebody famous had turned up and everyone was queuing to see them, but no, it was only the doctor and the needle. I must say though, that injection is the best I've ever had, just a scratch, it didn't hurt a bit. Now if I need an injection for say penicillin or anything I say " No thanks, I'll just have the smallpox one". My other favourite was the Polio vaccine on a lump of sugar, mind you I wasn't fussed about the vaccine, I would have been happy enough with just the sugar lump.

We knew we could rely on our doctors.

Chapter nine.

The beautiful rocking horse.

One of our favourite walks was across the fields. We were lucky because the farmer's fields had a public footpath through them and although they usually had cows in them, as long as we kept the dog close by us, they didn't bother with us. Mum, us three girls and the dog set off along the edge of the cornfield heading for the rickety bridge that lead into the farmer's field.

It was a chilly day and when we reached the bridge it looked a bit damp, but undaunted we climbed over the stile and leaned on the wooden rail to look at the river below. It wasn't a deep river but the water was flowing nicely as we had had some rain over the last couple of days. The bridge consisted of four planks of wood to walk on, a horizontal rail each side to hold on to, a vertical support structure in the middle and a stile at each end.

Mum instructed us to hold on tightly to the hand rails and walk carefully as the bridge was slippery. Well this bridge was lovely because if you jumped up and down on it, it shook, and being such a clever little person I ignored Mum's advice and started jumping. My sisters were annoyed with me as they were clinging onto the rails trying to keep their balance and walk across. I had almost reached halfway happily jumping away when my feet slipped from under me and I shot under the handrail and landed with a big splash in the river below, much to my sisters' delight. Poor Mum had to climb down the steep slippery bank to rescue me and help me up the bank. She carried me to my Nan's house with my sisters and the dog in tow. Nan lived about half a mile from the bridge and as it was uphill it was no easy task for Mum. By the time we reached Nan's I was so cold

I couldn't stop shivering and no amount of dry warm blankets and hot drinking chocolate made any difference.

I ended up in hospital with pneumonia. Our local hospital, as I have mentioned before, was only small and I ended up in the children's ward. In my ward there were just three cots with high sides on them, presumably to stop us little cherubs from escaping. In one cot was a girl of about the same age as me and in the other one a boy, younger than me.

Hospitals were very different then of course. For a start, once you were admitted to hospital it took you weeks to get out again. You had to eat all the meals "to build you up", in my case they would withhold my pudding until I had finished my main course. I bet Mum put them up to that, she knew I would do anything for pudding. Every day we had a fresh jug of water which we had to drink, all of it. Visiting was restricted to an hour a day, but that didn't make any difference to us as our Mum's couldn't get to see us very often anyway. The nurses were strict and the sister was a fire breathing dragon.

Every day we were wheeled in our cots out on to the veranda "to get some fresh air". That was an understatement. There we were, trapped in our cots for what seemed like hours while the wind whistled along the corridor like a hurricane. All the windows of course were wide open and by the time we were wheeled back into the ward we were frozen stiff with icicles hanging from our noses.

The one saving grace of this ward was that standing along the wall opposite was the most beautiful rocking horse I have ever seen. It was quite tall, about four feet, (Grandma can tell you), dapple grey with a long flowing white mane and tail. I used to gaze lovingly at it for hours, especially when a nurse told me that if I was good while I was in hospital I would be able to have a ride on it on the day I went home.

My first brush with sister came quite early on. The nurse handed me a steaming mug of hot chocolate to drink, probably to thaw me out after spending the day on the veranda, telling me to be very careful and not spill any. It wasn't my fault, it just slipped, and the whole lot covered my nice clean bed clothes. The bed had to be completely stripped.

As I started to get better and took more notice of my surroundings, I found I liked the girl in the other cot. Her name was Jean. The boy on the other side of me was a right pain, he would whinge and cry at the slightest thing, anyone would think he was ill or something. He used to have three injections a day plus other medicines throughout the day, and boy did he make a fuss. Mind you, by the time Jean and I had finished giving him the benefit of our older and wiser knowledge he used to scream every time a nurse came near him. In the end it took three nurses to give him an injection. We would tell him things like they had run out of small needles and they only had big thick ones left which were a bit blunt so the nurses would have to use a lot more force to stick them in. We told him he would probably choke on his tablets so instead of swallowing them he should suck them until they dissolved. I think my Mum would have been proud of me, she always said that if you were going to cry you may as well have something to cry about.

We were still all confined to our cots, which was boring, so Jean and I used to throw things to each other. The trouble was that neither of us were good shots and we frequently missed which meant one of us would have to climb over the top of our cot bars and retrieve it without sister or the nurses seeing us. We very often got our nightdresses caught on the metal catches on the cots in our hurry to climb over which meant we kept tearing them. On the rare occasions our Mums came to visit they would notice our torn nightclothes. We stuck together, Jean and I, and told them the nurses had torn them. Our Mum's used to go out muttering to the nurses to be more careful with us in future. The nurses just looked blank. We gave each other the thumbs up. Another success for us little people.

When I eventually escaped, sorry, was allowed to leave, I was so excited. I had been in hospital for about six weeks by then and I had dreamed of this day. Now was my chance to ride on the best rocking horse in the world. I was so excited I could hardly get dressed quick enough. But guess what? I never got to ride on the horse, but that whinging boy did, and he was smiling. What a terrible thing to do to such a sweet little person as me. I didn't get an explanation or an apology, just shoved out the door sharpish with my nightdress in a carrier bag. Life is so unfair, in fact I'm probably still traumatised by it.

Next time I end up in hospital, and there's bound to be a next time, I'm not going to be good, I'm going to scream at the top of my voice every time a nurse or doctor comes near me. I'll show them.

mum big sis and me   Dad relaxing

Chapter ten.

The Easter Parade.

We used to have an Easter Parade to church when I was at primary school. This one took place on a school morning after we had returned from our swimming lesson. As I may have mentioned before, we went to the local swimming baths in the mini bus that delivered our school dinners, after the dinner was unloaded of course.

After our lesson it was always a mad scramble to get dry, dressed and back on the bus. We were usually delayed because the swimming instructors had to fish those of us that had sunk to the bottom during our lesson out of the pool with the big fishing net. Me, being one of the sunken ones, had only seconds to dress before the bus left so it is fair to say I may not have looked my most attractive.

Once we arrived back at school we would rush into the cloakrooms and dump our swimming things on our pegs, or should I say place them tidily on our pegs? We would pick up our beautifully made palm crosses and dash back outside to form an orderly queue at the side of the road, with the girls at the front and the boys behind.

So there we all were standing in line in two's, waiting for the headmistress to give us the nod to start walking. Anyone passing by , seeing the state we were in, would not have been terribly impressed with what they saw I feel sure. Our half dried hair was not looking at it's best as none of us had a comb. Our school clothes were in disarray, our dresses were buttoned up wrong, our cardigans were inside out and a couple of the girls had the back of their skirts tucked into their knickers, much to the amusement of the boys. The boys had their shirts hanging out, one or two had their flies undone, their socks were all wrinkled and a lot of us had our shoelaces undone. But our enthusiasm had not been dimmed.

I even had my best sandals on, which would have looked really good except that my feet had grown so Dad had cut the toes out of them to allow me more room and now my brown woolly socks were bulging out of the holes.

This particular year we had a student teacher, Alice Take, or Miss to us children, who thought it would be really nice to have a donkey leading our parade to church. They are full of bright ideas aren't they, these student teachers? Luckily we had two donkeys in the village, a lovely docile old grey donkey who just plodded along happily taking everything in his stride. He had been a seaside donkey so had seen most things in his lifetime. The other one was a young brown lively donkey, full of high spirits and unpredictability. He either refused to move or went at a gallop, he did not do walking. The boys naturally chose the brown donkey to lead the parade.

The student teacher was put in charge of the donkey and when given the nod from the headmistress she gently pulled his reins. He refused to move. She tugged again and again but the only
thing that moved was his neck lengthening and his ears going back. As anyone who knows about donkeys will tell you, this is not a good sign. He would not budge. In the end the headmistress gave him a sharp whack on his rear end. That moved him. He set off at a gallop towing the student behind him and with us children running like the clappers to keep up.

Now, perhaps I should have mentioned this before, to get to the church we had to cross a main road, which fortunately wasn't very busy as we hardly had any cars then. The donkeys were stabled in a nice warm cosy barn just across this road, by the Red

Lion public house which was just to the left of the church. The man that owned them was the landlord of the pub. Have you noticed that the pub is always located close to the church?

We belted across the road, looking left, right and left again of course, and just as we thought he was going to gallop through the lichgates, he veered off sharply to the left and ran into the barn, followed by all us children. The other donkey glanced up at us as if to say "Oh I see you're doing the school run this year" and then went back to eating his hay. No matter how hard the student tried to persuade him to move back out of his stable, he would not budge. He was quite happy with his head in his bucket munching oats, all that exercise had given him an appetite. The headmistress surveyed the situation quietly and noticing that several of the boys were now engrossed in throwing straw at the girls she took control of the situation. She instructed the student to leave the donkey where he was, told us all to line up again and, with head held high, she marched us back out of the stable, across the road and into the church.

I can't say that the congregation were very impressed with us as we shuffled into church, dishevelled and covered in straw. Even the vicar, who must be used to strange sights, looked horrified as we filed into the pews to take our seats.

We sat through the service as still and quiet as we could although the straw was very itchy, and being children it made us scratch. I also realised as I sat there that when I had got dressed after our swimming lesson, in my haste, I had put my knickers on back to front and they were uncomfortable and I kept wriggling. I had also lost my clean handkerchief so I just kept sniffing. I can't tell you what the sermon was about because all that swimming, well, sinking in my case, and running had made me so hungry I was busy dreaming of our school dinner. I had my fingers crossed that it was sponge pudding and custard for afters. By the time we came out of church those of us that still had our palm crosses had shredded them to pieces.

For some reason we never had a donkey to lead the procession again, and we didn't get many student teachers after that either.

Willy and Dandy

With us 3 girls outside the village hall

Chapter eleven.

All Aboard.

On Ascension Day we always had a school outing which we children greeted with great excitement. Our Mums would come with us and all loaded down with our sandwiches for lunch we would board the bus. The buses were nothing like today's, they were slow and the engines seemed to have a whine to them. They didn't have a toilet. If you wanted air conditioning you opened the window. If you wanted music, you had to sing. We children were happy though, it was a day out of school, the sun was shining and we were off to the seaside. The teachers would make sure our crate of school milk was loaded on and after a head count the headmistress would take her seat at the front of the bus with the other two teachers, the driver would close the doors and away we would go. Our day out to the seaside meant we would be on the bus for a long time as we did not live near the coast. It must have taken us a good couple of hours to get there. As you know, not all children travel well and we would often have to stop because someone was feeling sick or needed the toilet. Eventually we would see the sea in the distance. Isn't it exciting when you get that first glimpse of the sea on the horizon? Once the bus was parked we would get our sandwiches out, the teachers would hand the milk out and we'd tuck in to our lunch. I think it is fair to say that the milk was a bit warm after the long journey but we drank it to wash our sandwiches down with anyway. Once we had finished eating we were free to go with our Mums to the beach or shopping or to the funfair. If we went somewhere like Great Yarmouth then we had a lot of choice as there was so much to see and do. The teachers would look after the children who didn't have a grown-up with them or some of the Mums would take an extra child with them. We all packed as much as we could into the time we had so that by the time we all got back on the bus for our homeward journey we had made sandcastles, paddled in the sea, eaten ice-cream, been shopping, eaten a stick of rock, been for several rides on the funfair, had some candyfloss, been for a donkey ride, had a drink of fizzy pop, petted the horses that stood patiently with their carriages waiting for customers, put a few pennies in the arcade machines and consumed the odd bar of chocolate and maybe a doughnut or two. I think you can safely say we were tired but happy as the bus headed for home. If you are thinking that some of us were sick on the homeward journey you would be wrong, we all were.

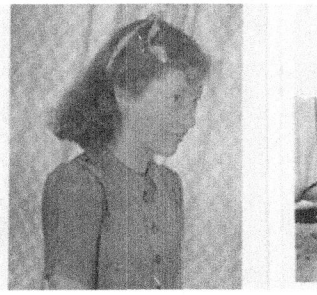

Aunty En   Aunty Dee and me

Chapter Twelve.

Can you come out to play?

As you probably realise by now, where we lived was surrounded by countryside so we had lots of options when it came to playing out, especially in the school holidays.

My best friend lived next door. This was extremely handy if it was cold out or if there was any doubt that she may not be coming out to play, as it meant I could just shout over the garden fence instead of having to brave the elements and go to the trouble of walking round to her house and knocking on the door, only to find out that she wasn't coming out. Our Mum had a very strict rule about people shouting out through open windows. Apparently she thought this was " very common" and we children were not allowed to do it, so of course we didn't, while she was around to see us.

On nice warm sunny days in the school holidays or at weekends, a group of us would take a packed lunch, either jam or fish paste sandwiches, a drink and an apple each, and off we would go over the farmer's fields. We would walk miles, ignoring the cows in the field, cows didn't frighten us country kids. One of our favourite places to go had a footpath through four fields and a river running through all the fields. We would go tree climbing, play hide and seek, or go paddling in the stream, turning the stones over on the river bed to see if any sticklebacks swam out. We would hang upside down over the bridges or just sit by the river. We would pick blackberries from the hedgerows to eat, or hazelnuts, or conkers which we would stuff in our pockets. One of our favourite games was being marooned on an island, well, over the river, or sometimes we would make a den in the woods. We would be gone all day, getting home starving hungry and filthy dirty, just in time for tea.

In the summer holidays once the corn had been cut and the straw baled we would play in the cornfields building tall towers out of the bales and daring each other to climb as high as we could before falling off. We would make long tunnels to crawl through out of the bales to reach a den we had made in the middle where we could sit and eat our lunch. We would build castles which we had to defend from the enemy, firing shots with our fingers or a stick if we could find one. It goes without saying that the farmer was not as enthusiastic about our games as we were and if we got caught we would get a right telling off and be sent home, but we would be back the next day to do it all over again. Our parents never worried about us being away all day, in fact they were probably glad of a bit of peace and quiet.

Don't get me wrong, we had our chores to do every day, school or no school. In our case we had the washing and wiping up to do every morning, the vegetables to prepare for dinner that evening, our animals to feed and care for and the table to set before dinner. One of our great delights was collecting frogs spawn in a jam jar from one of the ponds across the fields, just below the church, and bringing it home to watch as the first tadpoles hatched and then slowly transformed into tiny frogs. Quite magical.

In the same farmer's field was an enormous pear tree which was too tall to climb to get the fruit so we would spent hours trying to knock them off the branches with bits of wood we found lying around. This was quite hazardous really as five or six of us throwing sticks at the same time meant we were either getting bashed on the head by flying wood or scratched by branches as they were released. Mind you it wasn't worth complaining about when we got home as we weren't meant to be doing it anyway. The pears were only tiny and rock hard anyway but we still ate them as soon as we got them, no doubt getting tummy ache for several days afterwards as well.

The strange thing was that getting to the pear tree was difficult in itself. We had to climb down a very steep bank, we usually ended up sliding down on our backsides, splashing into the shallow stream at the bottom, and then having to haul ourselves up the bank on the other side and carefully negotiate the barbed wire fencing. It probably wasn't worth the effort, but year in and year out we did it. Oddly enough there were two other ways of getting to this tree, one by climbing the five bar gate and walking along the edge of the field, and the other one by walking along the side of the church, through the gate, along by the graveyard and along the edge of the field. I can never remember us going either of those ways, I guess we thought our way was more exciting. We weren't very bright were we?

At the other end of the village was the ford, well we had two in actual fact but the one further away was usually dried up. . In the summer there was only a trickle of water running across the road but in the winter it could get right up to the top of your welly boots. On one side of the road was a narrow wooden bridge with a handrail so you could cross the stream without getting wet. Very often my sister, my friend and myself would take the dog for a walk down by the ford and play happily on the little bridge for hours. Mum would always warn us not to get our feet wet which meant we would spend ages trying to push each other off the bridge and into the water. Once we had succeeded we then spent ages hanging our socks over the rail in the hope they would dry before it was time to go home. They never did. Eventually we would go squelching home. We always blamed the poor old dog, saying he had knocked us into the water until Mum threatened not to let us take the dog with us the next time to see if we still came back with wet feet. Our Mum was not daft was she? I wonder who I take after then?

There was a man, as I've mentioned before, in the village who kept horses. He rescued two seaside donkeys, as I'm sure you are aware, which my sister and I and an older girl in the village were allowed to ride. One was a young brown donkey and the other one was an old grey one. The brown donkey was a real handful to ride, as soon as you got on his back he was away and when you turned him towards home he ran like the clappers back to his stable. I couldn't control him so I used to ride the grey one who was a lovely gentle creature who would just plod along regardless of what the other one was doing. They were lucky to have found a nice home because along with the horses they were well loved and cared for by this kind man. I sometimes helped bring the horses in from the field by the church, he had old horses and a couple of heavy horses as well. To lead the heavy horses in I used to have to reach up really high to hold their halters, but they were gentle creatures. Sometimes in the summer the donkeys and one or two of the horses would be left out in the field down by the bridge. They had a big shelter if they needed it and the other girl who used to ride the donkeys lived next door to the field so she kept an eye on them.

Sometimes we would camp out, on the front lawn at home. Our "tent" consisted of two garden forks pushed into the ground at each end, the clothes prop threaded through the handles and a candlewick bedspread draped over the top. We had an old blanket to lay on and we would happily spend our time reading or colouring or spying on people walking past.

Mum had a job cleaning for some American service families when we were young, so in the school holidays we girls used to go with her. The families lived in the big manor house on the outskirts of the village, it had been made into flats where several families lived and also in the cottages in the grounds. The children did not go to our primary school, they caught a bus every morning to their own school. During the holidays we all played together climbing trees and riding our bikes around the grounds. I can remember the grounds being covered in snowdrops and then as soon as they had finished blooming it would be transformed into a sea of blue as the bluebells came out.

The manor house had an enormous front door which lead into the large hall which had two grand staircases, one on each side, leading to the upstairs flats. It looked really grand and I have always wanted a house with a grand staircase leading from the hall. I'm still waiting. The families had television and as a special treat we were allowed to sit and watch the children's programmes while Mum was cleaning.

The families were good to us children, and the children became our friends. Years later when we were all grown up, one of the families who we were especially close to came back to see us, we were even allowed to use the front room on that occasion. It was great to see them, especially our best friend Shirley Bathbun as my Dad used to call her. She still looked the same, a mass of ginger hair and glasses.

My big sister and I were lucky enough to go on holiday with our grandparents when we were young. Our younger sister, who is quite a bit younger than us (as she will tell you when you meet her) stayed at home. We usually went to Walton-on-the Naze, staying in a guest house in the town. We had a family room with four beds. The lady that owned the guest house also had a beach hut which we used for the week we were there. She would give us a packed lunch to take with us and on the first morning we set off in great excitement to find the beach hut amongst the rows on the seafront. My sister and I would race ahead searching until we found our hut, they had names rather than numbers and although I'm sure Nan and Granddad knew where it was they let us find it first. Inside we had a kettle, a gas ring, deckchairs and a small table so we really had everything we needed. We would get changed into our swimming costumes, grab our buckets and spades and head for the beach. Rad Nan and Granddad would settle in their deckchairs in the sun to read the newspaper while we built sandcastles or paddled in the sea. We would have our lunch in the hut and then return to the beach for the afternoon. At tea time we would head back to the guest house, on one occasion taking fish and chips wrapped in newspaper back with us. The landlady didn't mind, she soon found us some tomato sauce to go with them.

On the last afternoon we went to the shops to buy a small gift to take home for Mum and Dad, and then we went to the pier to play on the funfair. It was great fun with all the different rides and machines, all the lights and lots of noise. I loved the horses and the big wheel, especially when you stopped at the very top and swayed in the breeze. One of the last things we did was go in the House of Fun. You walked through in a long line holding onto the person in front as it was really dark inside. Every so often something would brush against your face, or jump out at you, or there would be a loud noise and frightening faces would light up to frighten you. The floor would go all spongy as you walked on it, or move, or a gust of cold wind would blow on your legs. I was the last person in the line, and I was petrified. I thought that at any minute something would come up behind me and grab me. While everyone else was shrieking with laughter I was screaming with fear. I screamed hysterically from the minute I went in until long after we came out safe and sound the other end. If you want to go on a ghost train, don't expect me to go with you. I don't do ghost trains or scary things like that. Yes, I know I'm a big girls blouse, but I can't possibly be brilliant at everything can I?

At home we would amuse ourselves in the garden playing with our rabbits, or spying on the bantams trying to lay eggs. We made mud pies in Mum's cast off baking tins and would leave them in the sun to dry. We would call for our friends and play marbles on the path, or "what's- the- time- mister- wolf?" and ball games on the unmade road outside our houses until someone would tell us to be quiet as they were trying to get their baby to sleep. We would go over the rec, as we called it, and play on the swings or slide, or play football, cricket, rounder's or rugby with the boys. We would spend ages trying to balance on the metal rails that run along the side of the road opposite the recreation ground.

On wet days we would take over the table in the living room and play with our farm animals, or with our Post Office, or with the type- writer one of us had been given for Christmas. Sometimes on a Sunday evening Dad would play hide and seek with us. He'd hide somewhere in the house in the dark and we'd go looking for him. When he jumped out at us we would run screaming our heads off back to the living room and slam the door before he could catch us. Poor Mum, it used to drive her mad and she knew we would all be too wound up to sleep that night.

I know you all now have this idyllic vision of us sweet little children in our ideal little world where everything was perfect, well I better put that right. My best friend, who I've mentioned lived next door, sadly lost her Mum when she was young and her Dad remarried a few years later. His new wife already had a son of her own and was anxious that he was included in our games. We girls would be in our shed playing hairdressers when the door would be flung open and this lad would be standing there holding his Mum's hand. She would say he wanted to play with us so she'd shove him in and close the door. We would try and ignore him for as long as we could but eventually temptation would get the better of us. When she came to collect him later he had a brand new haircut. I don't know what all the fuss was about, it grew back eventually.

When we were playing dressing up she would appear and insist he wanted to join us so we would dress him up in girls clothes, high heeled shoes and make up. She was not happy.

When we were going off to play in Farmer's Meadows for the day she insisted he wanted to come with us. He tagged along behind us and copied everything we did and tried to join in the best he could. We decided to play hide and seek in the last field in the afternoon, and sent him off to hide. We all then went home and left him there and wouldn't tell her where he was. It's fair to say none of our parents were too impressed with us that time, so we got sent to bed with no tea. In fairness to the lad I don't think he wanted to play with us anyway, it was his Mum who insisted. Angels we weren't.

On the outskirts of the village there was a small wood which in spring time was covered in a carpet of bluebells. We would either walk or bike there on nice fine days and spend ages picking the flowers. We would then go home with a big bunch each for our Mums as pleased as punch. They smelled gorgeous, the bluebells, not our Mums. Of course nowadays you're not allowed to pick them. The neighbouring village had a private wood full of daffodils, which we were not allowed in and certainly not allowed to pick. To get there you had to trek over several fields as well as the recreation ground at the back of Wim Nan and Granddad's without being seen by the farmer, apparently. They looked lovely in a glass vase on Nan's table.

Me with clockwise Auntie Rose & uncle George

Rad nan and grandad

Oh no, not chapter thirteen.

Don't swing on the gate.

At the end of our long garden path was the front gate. There was nothing outstanding or unusual about it, it was just a run of the mill wooden gate painted council red to match the front door. It consisted of two horizontal bars at the top with a gap in between just big enough for a little person to sit, if they were that way inclined.

The bottom half was made up of vertical bars with a gap of about three inches between them. (For those of you who are reading in centimetres, that's approximately the gap I am now indicating between my thumb and index finger). These were held in place with a thicker horizontal plank along the bottom which usefully had a narrow ledge on just wide enough for little feet to stand tippy-toe on. With me so far? Good.

We were forbidden to swing on the gate, the reason being that we might break it and then the council would have the expense of replacing it, and probably the world would end or something, well our playtime would anyway.

I had finished my lunch one sunny afternoon and I was hanging around by the gate waiting for my friend to finish hers and come back out to play. I had a good look around to see if I could see Mum, I couldn't so I was pretty confident that she couldn't see me, so I climbed on tippy-toe onto the ledge at the bottom of the gate and started swinging backwards and forwards. It made a lovely click as it swung onto the latch which I then undid so that I could repeat the process. Each time I swung a little faster and the click was getting louder as it slammed shut. I was having a wonderful time, as happy as a little person can be doing something they shouldn't. (Yes I am easily pleased). I unlatched the gate again and swung with all my might backwards and then forwards hearing the loudest click of all as the gate slammed shut. The gate shuddered to a halt but unfortunately my knee didn't and it slid between the narrow vertical bars and jammed solid, my knee, not the gate.

I tried tugging, twisting and lifting my knee with all my strength to release it but there was no way that it would move. It then dawned on me that the downside of not being able to see my Mum meant that she had no idea that her precious little child was in dire need of rescuing from the nasty gate. I tried shouting but that didn't help. So there I was standing on the gate, facing the road with my knee stuck fast. A considerable time later my friend came skipping round ready to play, but instead had to go and find Mum and explain where I was. I thought it strange that Mum hadn't spotted me earlier as usually she had this early warning radar when I'm doing something I shouldn't be.

Fortunately this gave me time to come up with a convincing story of why I was stuck because I just knew she was going to ask me. I told her I had seen a beautiful butterfly land on the top of the gate and I had climbed up to get a closer look at it but unfortunately my knee had slipped and the butterfly had flown away. I'd give her one of my most convincing looks followed by an innocent smile as I denied that I had been swinging on the gate. That's my story and I'm sticking to it, so don't you go telling any different, ok?

Mum pushed, pulled, tugged and shoved but my knee would not move. My friend even had a go but to no avail. The road we lived on was a very quiet road but on this particular day it was the very day that the midday bus ran and several of our neighbours were making their way back home laden down with heavy bags after going shopping in the local town. Of course everyone had a suggestion about how to get my knee out but after trying them all without success they got bored and wandered off to their own homes.

It was also the one afternoon a week that Auntie Dee came to visit. We girls looked forward to this day, a Tuesday if you really want to know, as Auntie would read us the story about the little Robin family in her weekly magazine. We preferred her version to Dad's as somehow all the animals ended up dead when he read it. She would have a cup of tea and a good old gossip with Mum, their tongues keeping up the same speed as their click-clacking needles as they knitted. Most importantly she would bring a packet of milk chocolate biscuits for us girls to share. She came on the midday bus and then she went back home on the same bus just before teatime. After exhausting all ideas of how to rescue me Auntie and Mum gave up and went indoors for a cup of tea. Even my best friend got bored and went off to play with some of the other children.

People wandered by every so often saying "Are you still here?" which was a bit silly really because if I wasn't they couldn't have asked me could they?". Nobody came up with an idea of how to release me. The most popular suggestion was to saw my leg off.

Mum and Auntie came out a bit later and had another go but without success so Mum said I would have to wait for Dad to come home and if he had to take the gate to bits I would have to pay for a new one. They then disappeared back in the house again, leaving me thoroughly fed up and feeling like a right ninny leaning on the gate.

Dad came home on his bike just before teatime and was both pleased and surprised to find me waiting by the gate. Mum soon told him why I was there so he wasn't quite so pleased after that. He leaned his bike against the hedge, knelt down, closely inspected my knee from all angles, stubbed his cigarette out and put it behind his ear, and then very carefully rolled my trouser leg up until it was just above my knee. He then gently pushed my knee which slipped out from between the bars. He was very clever was my dad. I obviously don't take after him.

At this very moment Auntie appeared, said "cheerio" to us all and set off down the road to catch her bus. I was stiff from standing for several hours, not to mention hot, thirsty and hungry, and my leg hurt when I tried to straighten it. I had missed the little Robin story, and when I limped back in the house I discovered that my sisters had eaten all the milk chocolate biscuits, every single one.

It didn't cure me of swinging on the gate, but at least I knew how to release my knee when it happened again. Hopefully if it ever happens to you, now thanks to me, you won't have to stand there for hours, and more importantly, you won't miss out on the chocolate biscuits. I can't think why my sisters were so mean, I had always been so kind and thoughtful to them.

Rad Grandad &Nan   Dad & Mum Wim Nan & Grandad

Chapter fourteen.

Never did me no harm.

I suggest that all of you of a nervous disposition skip this chapter because being of a sensitive nature you may find this upsetting. I'm going to talk about punishment. Depending on the severity of our misdemeanours we were punished accordingly, with the exception of the days when we would run poor Mum ragged and she would be at her wits end. Where is wits end? Have you ever been there? Is it nice? I just wondered. On these days we would get it big time. On these occasions we got the "Wait till your Father gets home" treatment. Why was he always Father when we were in trouble and not Dad? I'm not sure what was worse, the waiting for him or the punishment, it almost put me off my pudding.

Just stop for a moment and imagine three angelic little girls with shiny hair, clean noses, the sweetest little innocent faces with their little up turned noses, big trusting eyes, freckles, and big beaming smiles, wearing their prettiest frocks and shiny shoes, and you'll soon realise you are in the wrong house. We live next door.

There were days when we were naughty and we were not allowed out to play, and then there were days when we were naughty and sent out to play, we never quite knew which way things were going to go.

Another favourite punishment was sending us to bed without our tea. How cruel is that? Fancy starving us poor little children. Fancy depriving us of pudding. I might need counselling. Do they give you pudding after counselling? It was particularly cruel in the summer when we would lie in our beds listening to all our friends playing outside in the sunshine. We didn't dare get out of bed though because we knew as soon as we touched a toe on the ground Mum or Dad would hear us and come flying up the stairs. The thing with this punishment was it wasn't consistent, the one night I really wanted to be sent to bed without my tea I never ever was, and it was always the night we had liver and bacon. I hate liver and bacon.

Most of the time our punishment was sharp if not particularly swift. Mum favoured the word-slap method. I expect you were on the receiving end of it at times as well weren't you? It could become quite drawn out at times as she asked us a question, then answered it and then told you not to do it again. For any of you that haven't been at the receiving end of this I'll give you an example.

It went something like this. " How slap, many slap, times slap, have slap, I slap, told slap, you slap, not slap, to slap, do slap that?" slap. "More slap, times slap, than slap, I slap, care slap, to slap, remember " slap. Getting the idea ? It went on like this, but I'll let you fill in the slaps for yourself as I've had quite enough to be going on with, in fact it's made me feel a bit dizzy, I may need to go and lie down. "Do you ever learn?". "No you don't do you?". We never did learn, but always hoped we might one day.

Another good one was "If you don't stop that crying I'll give you something to cry for". And she did. My big sister was on the receiving end of this one quite a lot in the early days, can't think why.

Have you ever been knocked into the middle of next week and back again? Yes, me too. Can't remember what it looked like though, but no., it's ok I don't want to try it again.

I will confess that looking back on our punishment I think it was right, although at the time I thought we were hard done by. We soon learned that if we were naughty and got caught the punishment would hurt. It kept us more or less on the straight and narrow, it taught us that if you did wrong you would pay for it. It didn't stop us from getting into scrapes but it did stop us from getting into serious trouble.

We girls were expected to "Be seen but not heard". Fat chance. At school we would get the rule across or fingers if we were naughty, I only got it once for being cheeky to the dinner lady. You got called to the teacher's desk in front of the whole class and told to hold your hand out. I remember it mainly because it was my birthday and I felt a bit hard done by to get punished on that day. It hurt as well. Mind you, the boys got the slipper instead. Our school got through a few pairs of those I can tell you. We were always encouraged to "Tell the truth and shame the Devil", but it wasn't always the right thing to do. On one occasion my big sister and I went to the big pond. It was frozen at the time and Mum and Dad had told us not to go on it, so we did of course. My sister stepped onto the ice and it cracked and her foot went through it and her boot filled up with water. When we got home Mum asked her how she had got her foot wet and she made up some story about slipping in the stream. On this occasion I decided to "Tell the truth and shame the Devil" with the added bonus of getting her into trouble of course. I told them what had really happened and guess what? I got a good hiding for telling lies and trying to get her into trouble. It still hurts now. There's no loyalty between sisters. Perhaps I ought to bite her. What do you think? On second thought I better not, she's big enough to bite back now. The best thing to do was to shift the blame on to your friends in the hope that your Mum wouldn't say anything to their Mum. Little sisters were also good for blaming things on, and being little they got away with it. Probably the smartest thing to do is not get caught in the first place. Trouble is, you have to be clever for that to succeed, and as you have probably gathered by now, clever I ain't.

Mum often to used to say "This will hurt me more than it hurts you", but I'm still not convinced. Going without my pudding was torture.

Chapter Fifteen.
It doesn't matter what it looks like.

Clothes, as any girl will tell you, are very important. One of my earliest memories of just how important they are is of me standing in the middle of Mum's bedroom howling my eyes out. You see, I had grown.

Every summer and winter our clothes were swapped over. We took our summer clothes out of the suitcase that was stored under Mum's bed and put our winter ones in, and visa versa. On this distressing day it was our summer clothes that we were trying on. Last autumn I had carefully packed away my very favourite dress and now I was just trying it back on for size. It was beautiful, a white cotton dress with clusters of tiny blue stars, which Mum had made, and I used to wear it with a fluffy lemon coloured bolero, which Mum had knitted. It made me feel a million dollars when I wore it, and now it was too small. If I had known I wouldn't have eaten all those puddings during the winter. On second thoughts, I probably would have. My world had come to an end.   Mum made most of our dresses and knitted a lot of our jumpers and cardigans. Auntie Dee used to do quite a lot of knitting for us as well, she was really clever and could knit things like bunny rabbit or pussy cat borders to our cardigans, or embroider flowers on them, or make pom-poms. Back then clothes were more expensive to buy in the shops so most of ours were handmade. I seem to remember that a lot of our cardigans were beige or brown for some reason. Mum used to do a lot of smocking on the yolks of our dresses which was very clever and made them look really pretty, using different coloured threads to make intricate designs. Our dresses and skirts always had a "good hem" on to allow for us to grow taller, but unfortunately there was little room for expansion side ways, which with my love of puddings was a real shame. We always had a decent coat to wear, very often several sizes too big so that we could get plenty of use out of them. Clothes were handed down amongst the Mums when we had outgrown them, or taken to the regular jumble sales. Our shoes, as I have mentioned before were always "good" ones which we were measured for. We had brown strapped sandals in the summer which Dad would cut the top of the toes out of if our feet grew too much. Living in the countryside we always needed welly boots for splashing in the river and puddles.

Our hats and gloves were always hand knitted, they again were very pretty, especially our little bonnets with their colourful flowers embroidered over them. My big sister and I were usually dressed alike, there was only an eighteen month age gap between us, she usually wore blue and me pink for some reason. The strange thing is, the only socks I can remember wearing were brown woolly ones, summer or winter.

You would be right in thinking that we three girls were really well turned out, well almost right, two out of three were. Both of my sisters always looked neat and tidy and although my big sister and I were dressed alike I always managed to look like I had been "dragged through a hedge backwards". One of Mum's frequent remarks to me. They both had a natural grace about them which made them look elegant in whatever they were wearing. Me? Grace and elegance never came anywhere near me, not that it bothered me.

Our Mum had a brilliant way of persuading us that our clothes were just right. When we tried on clothes, particularly those we didn't like, she would ask us questions about them. Our clothes were always too big for us when we got them, to allow for us to "grow into them". It didn't matter that we could turn right round in them, or that the sleeves covered our hands, or that the hems were dragging on the ground. We would be asked the same questions regardless.

" Does it feel tight?". "Can you move in it?". "Is it pinching anywhere?". "Can you lift your arms?". "Does it feel comfortable?". We couldn't say no to any of those questions could we? Very clever.

If we said we didn't like it, or we thought it looked horrible the response we got was always "It doesn't matter what it looks like, it's how it feels"

I can remember on one occasion Mum buying my big sister and I matching trousers. I think they may have come out of the catalogue that one of our neighbours ran. You know the sort, where you paid a bit off them weekly. Sometimes that was the only way you could afford to buy new clothes. They were red tartan ones, thick and woolly, and I think they must have cost her quite a bit of money because the first time we wore them she wagged her finger at us and told us we had to take great care of them, as they had got to last us a long time. Off we went to play out in them, having promised to stay away from water and mud, and when we returned my sister's were still immaculate, mine had a big hole in the knee. We had only been out a couple of hours. I tried the "I fell over and hurt my knee" excuse but with no grazed knee to back this up it fell on deaf ears. Mum was not happy. I would have been sent to bed early except that it was a Wednesday which meant liver and bacon for tea. I have no idea how I managed to get a hole in those trousers. Perhaps the hole was there before? Perhaps someone else put it there. What do you think?   When we had photographs taken of us as children it was a big event because we had to go to the photographers studio.

Mum dressed us in our best smocked dresses and newly knitted cardigans, beige or brown, brushed our hair till it shone, no mean feat in my case, scrubbed our faces and dared us to play up. I must admit I even look cute in some of these photographs. Who said the camera never lies?

Chapter sixteen.

A trip to the dentist.

Our school dentist was a lovely man who always told us the same story on each of our six monthly visits. He had a donkey that for some reason he would take for a walk with his bicycle. The donkey decided one day that it wanted to go a different way, and being a donkey it did just that, and our dentist and his bike ended up in a ditch. Now, as I said, we got this story every time, but with a mouth full of sharp implements we were not in a position to say anything, but the chances are we wouldn't have said anything anyway as he was such a nice man.

If we needed a filling we didn't have the luxury of an injection beforehand. The dentist knew when he had hit a nerve because we jumped several feet in the air whilst emitting a piercing scream, knocking all the implements off the tray on the way. It used to take forever to drill a tooth then with those really slow drills that made your whole head rattle. You would lie back in the chair with your mouth wide open, while your brain shook, your teeth rattled and your eyes whirled around in their sockets. We ought to have worn goggles really, if only to stop our eyes from rolling across the dentist's floor never to be seen again. (Pun intended).

I have a theory about these drills which I can back up with evidence. I'm one of those unfortunate people who have more fillings than teeth which I'm sure has absolutely nothing to do with my sweet tooth, or my love of stodgy puddings. As you may have noticed in earlier chapters, I'm not terribly bright. My theory is that all that drilling loosened my brain cells and one by one they rolled out of my ears to be lost forever.

Okay, I admit I probably only had three in the first place, but it's still a great loss to me. I can back this theory up of course with hard evidence. My husband has only ever had one filling in his whole life, (yes, I'm really happy for him too) and he can answer those difficult questions that they ask those exceptionally bright youths on that television programme. Me, I don't even understand the questions and would probably get my name wrong as well.

I can remember when injections were first introduced at the dentists. He would say things like " This won't hurt a bit", which was either a lie, because it did, or the truth, because it didn't hurt a bit. It hurt a lot. He would always stand holding the syringe with it's six inch needle in full view of me while he squeezed about half the contents out into mid air. He would then say " Open wide" and like a blithering idiot I would. I felt sure that he would stick the needle in my gum and it would stick out the back of my neck. When the filling was completed he would say "Don't eat anything until it has hardened off", usually about a fortnight, and I would spend the rest of the day using sign language and dribbling because I had no control over my mouth. Nothing new there then!

I had better take a pause here because all that talk of injections has made me feel quite peculiar, I had better go and have a lie down.

In the meantime here's a true story to be going on with.

Mum was due home on the midday bus from her job in a grocery shop. Luckily it was a day when we had an afternoon bus back into town from the village we lived in. We girls were now "old enough to be sensible" while Mum was at work, added to which Rad Nan and Granddad lived close by to keep an eye on us. I think it will be beneficial to my defence to mention at this point, once again, that my sister is eighteen months older than me, and therefore should be a lot more sensible than me.

On this particular occasion I had been fighting with my big sister and I will own up to starting it. Anyway, we were chasing each other around the dining table when she grabbed my hand, and me, in my wisdom, decided to use my chin to bash her hand. Rather un-sportingly I feel, she moved her hand out of the way and I whacked my chin on the corner of the table, breaking one of my bottom teeth.

I decided the best way to play it when Mum came home was to be all tearful and put on my most convincing "victim" face, a well rehearsed look I may add. I practiced it in the mirror to make sure I had it spot on and I'm sure you would have been impressed with it. When she walked in, there I stood, this pathetic little child all tears and sobs clutching my broken tooth in my sweaty little palm. I held the tooth out to her and explained how I had slipped and hit my chin on the table, showing her the bruise that was now appearing on my chin, as I gazed at her with my sorrowful, tear filled eyes, only for my rat bag sister to pipe up "It was her own fault, she was fighting. All sympathy promptly packed it's bags and left the house. Mum was furious, she had got a thousand and one things to do that afternoon apparently, but instead she had got to rush round and catch the bus back into town to take me to the dentist. We caught the afternoon bus, which of course was full of people Mum knew, and who knew me, and of course she had to tell them all about it, especially the bit about going back into town after she had only just got home, and all because of me fighting.

Have you noticed how all Mum's have that same disapproving look? It's the sort of look that stops traffic. I think it originates in the delivery room when they are in labour. They've been in labour for about two days when the doctor appears and says " I don't want you to push yet, we're not ready".

We settled into our seats and trying to get her back on side I quietly asked "What do you think the dentist will do?". She gave me one of those withering looks that makes you realise that a), you shouldn't have asked and b), you weren't going to like the answer. She replied "With any luck he'll pull your head off and put it in a carrier bag".

Happily the dentist decided to leave the tooth as it was, saying that he would keep an eye on it , and deal with it if it caused any problems later on. It never did. I've still got it, it goes quite nicely with the rest or my appearance. If I smile you can see it, but I won't because I don't want to spoil you. I was happy but Mum wasn't because she had had a wasted journey, but at least she was now mad at the dentist which gave me a bit of a break

. Anyone seeing me on the home journey may have noticed a slight smile on my face, I was still wearing my head, it wasn't in a carrier bag in my lap. Mind you I wasn't smiling when Dad came home and asked Mum what sort of a day she had had. If only he hadn't asked.

At least Mum's day hadn't been dull and run of the mill. You would think she would have been pleased to spend all that extra time with her precious daughter wouldn't you? I bet she secretly wanted to thank me. I bet she looked back fondly on that day in years to come.

Chapter seventeen.

All stuck up.

One really hot summer it was so hot that the tar melted on the roads. We lucky girls were going on holiday with Mum, Dad and Auntie Dee. I suppose I was about nine then, my big sister would have been ten and the little one not quite two. We were very excited about spending a week in a caravan on a large campsite by the sea. We went somewhere really exotic, like Clacton or Walton-on-the-Naze.

We arrived at the campsite in the early afternoon and booked in and went in search of our caravan. The caravan was quite a big one, it had two bedrooms plus, once the table had been folded down and the cushions re-arranged, there was a further double bed. We hurriedly unpacked our cases in our bedroom and after having a cup of tea, and maybe a biscuit or three, big sis and I went off to explore the campsite while our little sister (who if you ever meet her, will tell you she's much younger than us) had her afternoon nap.

We had a good look round the campsite, we found the play area, the pond, the shop, the bike hire hut, the shower and toilet blocks, and finally the big entertainment hall where there seemed to be things going on most of the time. They had bingo, games, an amusement arcade, a big bar come eating area full of tables and chairs and a large stage where the evening entertainment took place. Satisfied that we had found just about everything we were interested in we decided to make our way back to our caravan.

I think I should point out at this point that we were wearing our brand new brown sandals, you know the sort. They were a pretty standard design, brown of course, they had a strap that threaded through a loop, and a buckle, a holey pattern on the top by the toes and thick cream coloured crepe soles.

We set off in search of our caravan, which was not easy as there was row upon row of identical ones stretching for miles. Eventually we found our way back, but I can't say Mum and Dad were terribly impressed when they saw us. You see we were two inches taller than when we set out, the melted tar had stuck firmly to the soles of our sandals.

Mum, Dad and Auntie spent ages scraping and scrubbing the soles to remove the tar, while we were "confined to barracks". Once they were satisfied that they had removed all the tar Auntie, who was obviously an expert on sticky sandals, suggested turning them upside down on the dustbin so that the hot afternoon sun could dry them.

After we had eaten our tea and washed and dried up, we got washed and changed into clean clothes as Auntie and Mum wanted to go to the Clubhouse for a game of bingo. We put our clean sandals on ready to go with them, but when we tried to move we found we couldn't, our soles were stuck firmly
To the linoleum, the sun had melted them and now they were a big gooey mess. With a huge tug from the grown ups we managed to lift our feet, only to find we still had the lino attached, we had ripped holes in the flooring. After more tugging the lino was removed and we were carried outside and set down on the path. The walk to the clubhouse was long and very slow, but our thighs and bums were nicely toned by the time we got there.

We found an empty table and settled down happily with our ginger beers and crisps with Dad, while Mum and Auntie went off to play a few games of bingo. After the bingo we all sat at the table and watched the entertainment on stage until we were so tired we could hardly keep our eyes open. It was time to wind our weary way back home to bed. We stood up but we couldn't move, we had stuck to the carpet. Fortunately they were carpet tiles, all brightly coloured in reds, blues, greens and purple, very pretty. The tiles lifted up easily and as everyone was really tired we shuffled back to the caravan with then still attached to our sandals.

Poor Dad was really concerned about the holes in the caravan floor, but he need not have worried because we repeated the process every night, and by the end of the week we had a good pile of carpet tiles in a variety of colours. Dad, being very clever (I don't take after him as you know by now), replaced the cold old lino with bright warm carpet tiles which I feel sure the caravan owner must have been delighted with when he saw them. My sister and I were delighted with our newly toned legs and bottoms, perhaps we should make a video?

Quite what the clubhouse manager thought of his " disappearing tiles" we will never know. Maybe he still has sleepless nights now, wondering where they went. Maybe he decided he wasn't cut out to be a clubhouse manager after all and joined the Navy. Who knows what became of him?

Us?   We went to a holiday camp in Cromer the next year and didn't leave our sandals in the sun to dry. We left Auntie at home as well, just to be on the safe side.

Me and big Sis on holiday

Chapter eighteen.

All washed up.

As you are probably well aware of by now I am a big help. In fact Mum often used to stand with her hands on her hips and say that a lot to me, so I must have been, mustn't' I? Mum's never lie do they?

During the school holidays I had a very important job every Monday. I was in charge of the copper, no not a policeman, the one we boiled the clothes in on washday, which was always on a Monday. Why? I have no idea but Monday was wash day, it must have been written in blood somewhere because it never deviated, even if it rained or snowed, the washing was always done on Mondays.

All the whites had to be boiled, you couldn't possibly put grey whites on the line, goodness me no, the neighbours would have looked down their noses at you. Once Mum had washed the whites they were put in a big mettle free standing tub, (the copper), the shape of a dustbin with legs, which was three quarters full of hot soapy water which Mum had switched on earlier to heat the water to boiling point. Mum had a pair of big wooden tweezers which she used to put the washing in the copper before putting the lid on it. These tweezers could cause a serious bruise on a big sister's nose if you were really lucky I discovered, quite by accident of course.

Anyway, here I am standing in the scullery, do houses have sculleries anymore? You don't seem to hear of them do you? Dad had painstakingly fitted some linoleum on the scullery floor when we moved in and it looked really posh. Have I mentioned he was really clever? My very important job was to watch the copper to make sure it didn't boil over onto the lino and spoil it while Mum went up the garden to hang out some of the other washing. There was just one teeny weeny problem with this, the scullery was right next to the pantry, and as you know, pantries are full of biscuits and cakes. I watched the copper as instructed, but it can be very boring so if you don't mind I'll just have a very quick peek in the pantry, just in case there happens to be any biscuits that are waiting to be eaten. Oops, that sounds like running water. I run to the back door and yell, "Mum, the copper's boiling over". Mum drops everything and runs down the garden path like the clappers to rescue the situation. After we've mopped up and I've been given a stern lecture on not taking my eyes off the copper, a finger wagging Mum retraces her steps up the garden. Our garden is quite large, Dad has worked hard digging it to grow vegetables in, he laid the paths, put the washing lines up and even whittled a couple of garden props out of a tree trunk. Now look what you've made me do, I was so busy describing the garden to you that the copper has boiled over again. "Mum, the copper's boiled over". Sprint, sprint, mop, mop, lecture, lecture.

It's hungry work this copper watching, I'll just have another peek in the pantry, I haven't looked in the cake tins yet. I'll take a knife, just in case there's my favourite sponge in one of them. I start opening the tins, fruit cake no, rock cakes no, dead fly buns no. Ooh Victoria sponge with chocolate butter cream filling, yummy. I've just taken a bite, is that running water I can hear? "Mum, the coppers boiling over" Sprint, sprint, mop, mop, lecture, lecture, finger wagging.

I've got a bit of a dilemma now, lurking in the cake tin is a half eaten piece of Victoria sponge. If Mum finds it she will know I've been helping myself. It's no good, I'll have to eat the evidence, I won't be a minute. Be a dear and watch the copper for me. Is that running water? "Mum……" Sprint, sprint, mop, mop, lecture, lecture, followed by a hefty left handed clip round the ear. By the end of the summer holidays Mum had knocked several seconds off her sprint time and could hurdle the garden props without breaking her stride. She had also dropped two dress sizes. She should have made a video shouldn't she? I feel sure that if she hadn't been so out of breath she would have thanked me for that. See, I said I was a big help.   Gardens, as I'm sure you are aware, can be dangerous places. Have you ever been struck on the head by a frozen sheet? I have. It's a bit like being struck with a tin tray, yes I've experienced that as well. You should never turn your back on a clothes prop either, they stand there looking all innocent but the minute you walk past they slip and crack you on the top of the head with such force that you fall face down in the garden that your Dad has just sown his vegetable seeds in. So not only have you got a sore

head and a dirty face, but you've got a sore bottom as well because Dad saw you land in the newly sown plot and thinks you did it on purpose. As you're now covered in mud, you're in trouble with Mum as well. Whoever said that childhood was fun didn't live in our house.

    That's enough fresh air for now I had better go back indoors. The washing is now finished thank goodness, how Mum manages on her own when I'm at school I'll never know, I bet she misses me. There is a downside to all this helpfulness, all that steam. I know it is brilliant for my complexion, my pores are all sweated out. It even clears up some of my spots, but it has made my curly hair into a massive ball of fuzz and even I have to admit it   looks ridiculous. My job is done for the day, and an excellent job at that, even if I do say so myself. If I'd waited for anyone else to say it I'd still be stood there now. I am now free to go out to play, looking, as Mum would fondly and frequently say, "like I've been dragged through a hedge backwards".

One thing I discovered very early on in my life was that boys don't like girls with wild frizzy hair. Mind you, they discovered quite early on in their lives that they didn't like being punched on the nose, apparently.

Chapter nineteen

Anyone for Christmas cake?

Yes, it's that time of year again, or soon will be. It's time to make the Christmas cake. No it's not just a case of opening packets and shoving all the ingredients in a bowl and mixing together, or horror of horrors, buying one from a shop.

It all starts with the mixed fruit, all the raisins, sultanas and currents have to be de-stoned and all their stalks have to be taken off, one by one. Once Mum was satisfied that we had removed all the stalks she washed the fruit thoroughly and dried them in a clean tea towel. After this they were spread onto a tray and carefully laid in the airing cupboard for a couple of days to make sure they were nice and dry. Seems straightforward enough doesn't it?

As you know, it can be quite chilly out at this time of year and the airing cupboard is nice and warm and cosy. My sister's black and white cat, Cuddles, thought so too. Even though she wasn't allowed in the airing cupboard it never stopped her from getting in there and sleeping for hours on end. She looked so cute nestled amongst the sheets and towels snoring gently with that little grin on her face
that all happy cats seem to have. Have you ever tried to remove a cat from it's favourite place when it doesn't want to be removed? They don't come quietly do they? Cuddles was no exception.

First, she would open one eye and look around, then the other eye would open and we would get the steely glare. As you slowly moved your hand towards her she would uncurl her paws and reveal her sharp claws. One set of sharp claws would be used to fend you off while the other three sets embedded themselves in the towels she was lying on.

We just had to make a grab for her and hope for the best. The thing is, she would come out of the encounter unscathed, while we got ripped to shreds and Mum's towels looked more like Venetian blinds by the time we had finished.

We would look like we had gone three rounds with a lion instead of the family pet. Our hands and arms would be covered in scratches, which meant Mum would get the iodine out, and our clothes would be torn to shreds. Eventually we would get her out, she would wander off with her head held high and a flick of her tail just to let us know that she was not impressed, and then we could carefully place the fruit on the shelf on top of the towels.

The really tricky bit now was keeping Cuddles out of the airing cupboard. She would lurk around the door awaiting the opportunity to dash back in again. Mum would shriek "Don't open that door", and I'm sure we never did, but when we went to get the fruit out a couple of days later, there was the cat curled up contentedly on top of it purring away with her eyes closed and her lips forming a satisfied little grin and we had to start the whole Cuddles removal process all over again, but not before wearing Dad's big leather gloves, crash helmet and goggles to give us some protection. I wouldn't mind but the iodine was still stinging from the last session. We managed to get most of the hairs out of the fruit, well, the white ones anyway, the black ones were harder to find. Along with the chopped cherries and mixed spices they went into the mixing bowl and with Mum's help we all stirred the mixture and made a wish before putting it in the cake tin, that Dad had carefully lined, and into the oven. It seemed to take ages to cook, hours in fact. Mum kept a close eye on it, we weren't trusted with that bit. The trouble was, if you opened the oven door too soon the cake would sink in the middle. If that happened then we would have to start all over again, and disturbing Cuddles more than twice in one year was not a good idea. She would not be happy.

Once the cake was cooled and stored for a couple of weeks Mum would coat it in apricot jam and put the marzipan on. I love marzipan. I always hoped Mum would roll it out thinly so there would be loads left over, but there never was. Then the big day arrived, it was time to make the icing. No, it didn't come ready made then, we had to mix the icing sugar with egg white and a dash of lemon juice. The trick was to get it to the right consistency, either so it formed peaks, for rough icing, or slightly runnier so you could smooth it on to the cake. Mum and both my sisters are good at icing cakes. Mine just look as though I had slopped the icing on any old how, can't think why.

I know what you are all dying to ask. Did we get all the cat's hairs out? I've no idea. I don't like Christmas cake so I never ate it. Any visitor that tried it never commented on it being a bit hairy, but then again we never told them what had happened. Sometimes ignorance is best,

The Christmas puddings would also be made weeks before Christmas. Once Mum had made them, upsetting the cat in the process, it was my job to keep an eye on them while they were cooking. As you know, the mixture was poured into a small pudding basin, greaseproof paper was put on the top, and then a piece of muslin was tied tightly around the top to stop it from escaping, before placing the basin in a saucepan of water on top of the Rayburn. It used to take several hours for them to cook and this was where I came in. My job was to make sure that the saucepan did not boil dry and burn the saucepan.

It was very pleasant whiling away your time in front of a nice warm Rayburn on a cold day and, being a child that felt the cold, it should have been a happy experience. If I have any faults, and I'm pretty sure I don't, my concentration may lapse occasionally, through no fault of my own of course. I would be busy playing marbles on the floor with my big sister and having just lost my last marble to her I would remember to check the saucepan. I would lift the lid carefully hoping to see steam coming out but oh dear, all I could see was smoke. "Mum, I think the saucepan needs topping up" I would yell helpfully and hopefully at the top of my voice. I would give her one of my best smiles when she entered the room, but to no avail. She would fetch a new saucepan of water, clip me round the ear and tell me not to let it happen again. It's very tiring watching saucepans you know, and being in such a warm and cosy place is it any wonder that small girls nod off? It was only for a couple of seconds, in fact I'm pretty sure it was no longer than a blink, honest. "Mum, I think the saucepan needs topping up". I give a cheeky smile, get a clip round the ear, and off Mum goes in search of yet another saucepan. So as not to fall asleep again I am now sat at the table playing with our farm. I've put the hedges up, the cows are all mooing contentedly in the field, the little lambs are all scampering about, the horses are all looking over the stable doors, the dog is sat by the pond watching the ducks swimming round in circles, the chickens are scratching and clucking away in the yard and the new tractor is standing majestically in the new barn. Now look what you've made me do, I was so busy describing the farm to you that I forgot all about the pudding. It's your fault this time, not mine, but I bet it will still be me who gets the clip round the ear. Fancy distracting such a sweet little person from their job like that.

"Mum, I think the saucepan needs topping up again". Biggest smile yet. Mum lifts the saucepan up, leaving the pudding basin still sitting on the hotplate. She peers at me through the big hole in the bottom of the saucepan. It is not a happy face looking at me, I can feel another ear clipping coming my way. Did I mention my Mum was left handed? At times like this I wish she would let her wild side out and use her right hand on the other ear for a change because, to be quite honest with you, my left one is beginning to sting a bit. Please don't mention this to her because she'll reach for the iodine bottle again.

This time Mum has to go and borrow a saucepan from one of the neighbours. For some unknown reason I am relieved of pudding watching duties. I didn't even get a thank you. I think she was just too busy to remember and I'm sure she couldn't have managed without me. I bet I will be her first choice next year for pudding watching duties. She quite often says I'm a lot of use, and that's praise enough for this little person.

You may be wondering if the Christmas puddings suffered at all, I've no idea, I don't like Christmas pudding either, you'll have to ask my big sister. If you're interested, I like treacle sponge pudding with custard, or evaporated milk. Just thought I'd mention it, in case you get the urge to make one and happen to have a portion or two to spare.

Chapter twenty

Christmas times past.

I have fond memories of my childhood Christmases, well apart from plucking chickens. Now I will admit to being a whimpette where my meat is concerned. Although I was bought up in the countryside I like my meat heavily disguised. To me those lovely creatures I see lolloping around the fields are completely different to the ones served up on my plate at mealtimes.

As a child though I can remember our meat came wearing it's coat, or feathers, and Christmas was no exception. I can remember the chicken we had for Christmas dinner arrived all floppy necked and footed, but it's eyes were watching me accusingly wherever I went. Yes, it was dead, but I guess no-one had told it's eyes yet.

Mum would sit us all round the table so that we could pluck the feathers off. Every time I grabbed a handful it's little eyes would glare at me. The feathers were put in a box and probably used to stuff a pillow with at a later date. Once the poor little thing was wearing nothing but it's Birthday suit I would make myself scarce because then it got really gruesome. Mind you, served up on Christmas day with stuffing and gravy it tasted delicious. We would have Dad's home grown Brussels sprouts, which to be honest I didn't like, to me they are just punishment on a plate.

While I was allowed to pick the vegetables out of the garden I was not allowed to pick the Brussels. It might have something to do with the fact that, as I've mentioned before I only ever found four at one time, one for each of them, whilst putting on my sweetest grin and saying "I don't mind going without". It never worked, I always ended up with twice as many as anyone else. We would all sit round the carefully laid table with our party hats on while Dad carved the meat and Mum served the vegetables and stuffing out. If we were really good we could be trusted to help ourselves to the gravy, mine always landed on the tablecloth.

We used to make our paper chains to decorate the living room ceiling with and unpack all the precious tree decorations which had been carefully put away after the last Christmas. We always had a real Christmas tree with roots which every year we would plant out in the garden afterwards, but they never grew. Rad Nan and Granddad had more success though and one of theirs grew to about forty feet high, which was a shame really as they had planted it right outside their back door and it blocked out all the light in the kitchen.

On Christmas morning we used to visit our grandparents who lived in the village to exchange presents. The grown ups would usually have a sherry and mince pie while we girls played with our new toys. One year Auntie Dee was with us and just after we arrived at Nan and Granddads her favourite radio programme started, you know the one, all about simple country folk. She told us we had to sit still and be quiet while she was listening to it, on Christmas morning of all mornings! We did sit still for the whole ten minutes, and we didn't make a sound, we just sat under the table and tied her shoe-laces to the leg of her chair.

We girls were bought up not to tell lies, so some of the time we didn't. Dad, on the other hand used to tell us a whopper every Christmas. No, not about Father Christmas, we knew that was Dad because one year he dropped the sack of presents on his foot and he used words that I'm sure would have made the real Father Christmas blush. He hoped we girls were asleep and didn't hear these words, but of course we were only pretending to be asleep.

He used to lie about the Christmas pudding. Every year without fail as the pudding was being served up he would tell us that one piece had some money in it. Even though we grabbed his dish and mashed his pudding into tiny bits he somehow managed to find a sixpence, a two bob bit, or a half crown in his piece of pudding.

On Christmas evening our other grandparents would arrive and we would spend the evening all sat round the table, playing cards or board games like Snakes and Ladders or Dad's favourite, Ludo with much noise and laughter. Dad never ever won Ludo, Auntie Dee always insisted he hadn't thrown a six and pushed all his counters back to the start. The grown ups would have a drink, brown ale or mild for the men and a glass of sparkling Perry or sherry for the ladies. Us girls would have our ginger beer and crisps. Bliss.

Our Nan was the caretaker and dinner lady at our primary school, as you already know, and every year she would put a shiny new sixpence in each child's Christmas pudding. What would health and safety have to say about that now? We all survived.

One year a group of us children in the village thought it would be nice to go Carol singing. We borrowed a paraffin lamp from a neighbour, promising faithfully to take great care of it, and gave it to the most sensible one amongst us to look after, not me obviously. We set off one cold and frosty evening wrapped up warm and full of enthusiasm. The problem was, we only knew a couple of verses of the Carols so we would sing a couple of lines really slowly and then knock on the door, hoping that the door would be answered and money put in our tin quickly before we ran out of words. We had gone about half way round the village, our confidence growing, when the mishap occurred. The boy holding the lamp tripped up the curb and fell over. The paraffin lamp went crashing to the ground and smashed. That was the end of our Carol singing, we all went home stinking of paraffin , much to our parents horror, and every penny we had collected had to be spent on a new paraffin lamp.

One year I had a brand new doll for Christmas. She was all wrapped up in a soft yellow blanket. She was meant to replace the doll that I had whose head and arms kept falling off and that Auntie Dee had repaired on numerous occasions. It didn't work. I took the nice blanket and wrapped my old doll in it and discarded the new one. I still have that doll today only these days I do the repairs. Her arms and legs are stuck on with masking tape and her head is kept in place with a pencil and more masking tape. She really is beyond repair, but she's not going anywhere. Just as well really as bits might drop off if she does.

Mum and Dad always tried to buy us a decent present each, probably paying for it in weekly instalments as was usual in those days, and then we would get clothes, books, tins of toffees and big tubes of sweets. Mind you the sweets weren't so popular with Mum and Dad the one year that my sister (who's old enough to know better), shook the tube upside down and the lid came off and all the chocolate sweets covered the bed. It was two o'clock in the morning, and Mum and Dad had only just gone to sleep. Father Christmas was not happy.

Christmas seemed to be more about the fun than the presents then. Having a good time with all the family, playing silly games, like Blind Mans Bluff, and having a real laugh. Probably not allowed to call it that now. Mind you, the sweets were nice, although mine didn't last as long as everyone else's. Neither have my teeth.

It always seemed to be more about the family having a good time than whether your best friend got better presents than you did. Of course we weren't brainwashed with advertisements like children are today, I think we were just grateful to get anything, especially me, as Father Christmas always seemed to know if I'd been naughty. It was amazing I ever got any presents.

Granddad

Chapter twenty one.

Up the garden path.

Our house had a very long, straight footpath leading from the front gate, past the side of the house and then turning sharply to the left to reach the back door. All along the right hand side was a low privet hedge, we kept it low so that we could see what the neighbours were up to, and just as the path turned a sharp left Dad had planted his prize blackcurrant bushes at right angles to the privet hedge. The blackcurrant bushes looked nice in the summer and were always laden down with fruit. Mind you, as it was one of our jobs to pick all the little blighters every year so Mum could make jam, pies and crumbles with them, I may not have appreciated them quite as much as Dad. Fortunately for me summer was well past and we were now in the depths of winter.

Being such a helpful child, as I'm sure you have realised by now, I decided to clear the snow from the path so that when Dad came home from work he would be pleasantly surprised. It was no mean feat I can tell you, as I've already mentioned, the path was long, probably three miles long at least, although I'm not terribly good at judging distance.

I got to work with the big broom and several buckets of hot water, sweeping and sloshing away for what seemed like hours until I was satisfied that I had got all the snow off, leaving a nice clear path for Dad and his bike. It was very tiring work and as Dad wouldn't be home for a couple of hours I went indoors for a rest feeling really proud of myself.

Just before Dad came home I positioned myself in front of the blackcurrant bushes so that I had a clear view of the gate at the far end. There I stood, glowing in anticipation of all the praise Dad would heap on me when he saw my handy work. Things like "What a wonderful surprise", or "Wow you've done a really good job", or maybe "You're the best daughter a father could have".

As Dad came into view I smiled and waved gaily at him and although by this time it was getting really chilly, and the light was fading, I decided to wait until Dad reached me before going back into the nice warm house.

Dad arrived home on his bike, wearing his blue woolly hat, him, not the bike , his cigarette stuck firmly to his bottom lip as usual, and waved back to me before getting off his bike and opening the gate. He managed to take a couple of steps before his legs shot up in the air and he fell flat on his back, still holding onto the handlebars of his bike. He gallantly struggled back up and leaned on the bicycle saddle whilst executing a series of kicks and flicks, his legs moving like greased lightning. He finished this display with a dazzling spin whilst twirling his bike like a dance partner before coming to rest in the privet hedge. Undaunted, he picked himself and his bike up and, muttering words I'd never heard before, but have several times since, he treated me to yet another display of fancy footwork, which I am sure would have won him first prize in any dance competition, before ending up doing the splits. I think by the look on his face he was even more surprised than I was at this.

It took him a bit longer to recover from this but once he did he spent almost two seconds upright before his feet shot up in front of him and he slid with great speed and not too much, if I'm being picky, grace into the blackcurrant bushes followed closely by his bike. He lay there with his feet in the air, his cigarette still firmly stuck to his bottom lip and with his blue woolly hat at a jaunty angle over one eye. Me? I made a hasty retreat.

In my defence M'lord, no-one told me it wasn't a good idea to clear paths with hot water on very cold days. Did I have any climate change lessons at school? No. How was a not very clever little person like me to know that water turns to ice when it's very cold? I blame the teachers.

I think I can safely say that when Dad finally caught up with me I couldn't sit down for a week, but in all fairness it took Dad a lot longer before he was able to sit down comfortably.

The happy outcome was that the blackcurrant bushes benefited greatly from their pruning, we had a bumper crop the next year. Unfortunately I had to pick all the little blighters on my own. I think I'm going to give up being helpful from now on, well until the next time anyway.

As I shall be off to Big School soon, or to give it it's full title, Technical and Modern School, perhaps I ought to "turn over a new leaf". The school title has since changed, mainly because trying to write that on your exercise books took up a lot of space and ink. Needless to say I didn't get in the Technical side, although a friend of mine did, the smarty pants. Still I had a new satchel, a uniform that I might grow into before I leave school, and I'm armed with all my qualifications, a width swimming certificate and a tie 3rd high jump certificate. I 've already spent the six pence on sweets. I feel I'm destined for greatness, don't you?

……………………………............…

Granddad's Poem.

My adored Granddad used to bounce me on his knee while reciting this and then drop me in a heap on the floor at the end. Great fun. Thanks to Auntie Dee for writing it out for me as I had forgotten it……

There was an old man, he ran mad,
He jumped into the pudding bag,
The pudding bag was so full
he jumped onto the roaring bull,
The roaring bull was so fat
he jumped into the gentleman's hat,
The gentleman's hat was so fine
he jumped into the glass of wine,
The glass of wine was so clear
he jumped into the barrel of beer,
The barrel of beer was so thick
he jumped onto the walking stick,
The walking stick woke, and gave him a poke,
And sent him home on the nanny goat,
The nanny goat ran so fast he fell flop upon the grass.

A few thank you's.

This book is about my early years living in a small Essex village. I have left a few clues as to the village I grew up in, it's still there, they haven't demolished it yet, but then again they haven't read my book yet. I hope you manage to track the village down but sorry, there is no prize for doing so.

I have a long list of thank you's to make, and I apologise now for the one's I miss out. Mum and Dad sadly are no longer with us but I owe them the biggest thank you of all. I had a great childhood, but their view may have been different. My two long suffering sisters who surprisingly still speak to me, for all the laughter we've shared over the years, and I hope we will continue to see the funny side of life for a long while yet. My Aunts and Uncles for all their patience and love, not to mention chocolate biscuits. My two wonderful sons to whom I have been a constant embarrassment, and will continue to be for a good while yet. I hope. My beautiful step daughter and her lovely family. My lovely daughter in law for bringing a bit of sanity into the family, and all my precious grandchildren, who with any luck will follow in grandma's little footsteps, causing chaos where ever they go.

Special thanks go to my long suffering husband David who has put up with me hogging and swearing at the computer, sorted all my photographs for me, fixed the computer when I've messed it up, dealt with my temper tantrums and been a thoroughly good egg. He may have lost all his hair, but I'm sure that can't have been my fault as well. To all my outlaws who I'm sure mutter "you can choose your friends, but not your relatives", several times a day.

Last but not least a great big thank you to Jane who was the one to encourage me to write this book. It's all her fault, not mine.

Just remember as you go through life's twists and turns, life is fun and there's a lot to laugh about.

Mum and Dad with us three girls on their

Golden Wedding